# The Golden Age of Normandale

Also by Willie G. Moseley

*Classic Guitars U.S.A.* (1992)

*Stellas & Stratocasters* (1994)

*Executive Rock: A Fan's Perspective on the Evolution
of Popular Music Since 1950* (1996)

*Guitar People* (1998)

*Bill Carson: My Life and Times with Fender Musical Instruments*
(with Bill Carson, 1998)

*Vintage Electric Guitars: In Praise of Fretted Americana*
(with Bill Ingalls Jr., 2001)

*Heart of Dixie: Everyman Observations from a Transitional South* (2006)

*Smoke Jumper, Moon Pilot: The Remarkable Life
of Apollo 14 Astronaut Stuart Roosa* (2011)

*The So-Called Commentaries, Vol. 2: Everyman Observations
on Reality, Entertainment, and Politics* (2011)

*Forever Blue: The Memoirs of a Lanier High School and University
of Kentucky Coach* (with Bill Moseley, 2013)

*Peavey Guitars: The Authorized American History* (2015)

*The Bass Space: Profiles of Classic Electric Basses* (2018)

*The Atlanta Rhythm Section: The Authorized History* (2018)

*Bakersfield Guitars: The Illustrated History* (2021)

*Basses and Guitars: The Huckabee Collection* (2022)

*A Luthier's Life: The Guitar Odyssey of Roger Fritz* (2023)

*Thunder Out of Texas: The Illustrated History of Robin Guitars* (2025)

# The Golden Age of Normandale

## An Illustrated Remembrance of Montgomery's Legendary Shopping Center

# WILLIE G. MOSELEY

PRINCIPAL PHOTOGRAPHY BY
PAUL ROBERTSON SR. AND JOHN ENGELHARDT SCOTT

FOREWORD BY DAVID L. ROBERTSON

BLACK BELT PRESS
MONTGOMERY

Black Belt Press
105 S. Court Street
Montgomery, AL 36104

Cataloging-in-Publication Data

ISBN 978-1-961938-24-3

Unless otherwise noted, all photos are courtesy of the Paul Robertson estate or the John Engelhardt
Scott collection at the Alabama Department of Archives and History. Images of newspaper ads,
logos, and photos accompanying press releases or captioned as press releases are from *Montgomery
Advertiser* and *Alabama Journal* issues catalogued at www.newspapers.com unless the captions
indicate otherwise.

Design and composition by Randall Williams

Printed in the United States of America

BLACK BELT PRESS | MONTGOMERY

*The Black Belt, defined by its dark, rich soil, stretches across central Alabama. It
was the heart of the cotton belt. It was and is a place of great beauty, of extreme
wealth and grinding poverty, of pain and joy. Here we take our stand, listening to
the past, looking to the future.*

*Once again, this is for the Missus—*
*life partner, soul mate, and best friend.*

# Contents

# Foreword

David L. Robertson

To say that Willie G. Moseley is unique is an understatement. Let me take you back in time to 1957.

Beaumont Drive was filled with new brick one-story homes with concrete driveways and accompanying carports. Our block had a good number of boys who would gather in the Moseleys' back yard for a game of baseball or touch football. Willie—who we knew as "Billy" before he became a rock star writer—would often be distracted by the path of a bumblebee or the coloration of a leaf. I recall his extensive collection of butterflies as well as an assemblage of bubble-gum football cards. Billy had memorized factoids from those collections that he would quote to willing listeners. These obsessions would later be replaced by accumulations of guitars and NASA memorabilia.

How many of you with gray hair (or no hair) have kept up with childhood friends? It's not that easy. Two roads may diverge in a distant wood, but high school, college, military service, marriage, children, and other incidentals along the way create so many routes of destiny, it is difficult to recall the events of yesterday.

And time has brought Willie and me back to a new intersection in our lives.

For my personal enjoyment, I had saved a box of 4 x 5-inch negatives of events and people that my father had photographed at the new Normandale Shopping Center circa 1954–1962. Converting these negatives to positives is not that complicated in our digital world.

Over the years, I have read a lot of Billy's/Willie's deep insights related to people in Alabama. The "flash bulb" in my mind ignited with the thought that Willie could put together facts for the Normandale visuals that filled in the gaps.

My friend Willie G. Moseley's NASA mission-like determination has gone above and beyond my expectations.

# Acknowledgments

Grateful appreciation is expressed to the following individuals for their assistance and/or sharing their recollections and images (alphabetical order):

Owen Aronov, David Azbell, Vicki Baker, David Bamberg, Michael Bird, Delores Boyd, William "Sonny" Bozeman, Suzanne Sisson Burroughs, Amelia Chase, Barry Chrietzburg, Mary Sue Stagner Clark, Michael Cohen, Foster Dickson, Nancy Evans, James "Scooter" Fenton (R.I.P.), Rubin Franco, Tommy Giles, Julia Hightower Gregg, Rusty Gregory, David Herman, Michael Herman, Stanley Herman, Heather Hutto, Jane Laseter (R.I.P.), Frank Litchfield, Tom McCabe (R.I.P.), Dick McAdams, Leah Larson Meacham, Junie Pierce, Laurens Pierce, Frank Potts, Barney Roach, David Robertson, Paul Robertson Jr., Bill Scott, James Scott, Mary Jo Scott, Lisa Segall, Arrol Sheehan, Judy Herman Shujman, John Shryock, Lisa Stanton, Tommy Thompson, Jim Turner, Roger Tyus, Mrs. Jim Vann, Diane Walker, Desmond Wingard (R.I.P.).

Special thanks to Julianne Eaker and George Howell for their social media liaison efforts.

Invaluable information was utilized from these periodicals, organizations, and government agencies:

*AL.com,* Alabama Department of Archives and History, Alabama Department of Public Health, *Alabama Gazette, BOOM—River Region,* Easterseals Alabama, *INDY Magazine, The Montgomery Independent, Prime Montgomery, and* Tallapoosa Publishers, Inc.

A tip of the headstock to Glenn Mackey, Colonel, USAF (retired), for his now-standard pre-submission perusal, suggested edits, and corrections.

Likewise, the Messrs. Spilman get their now-standard "read-between-the-lines" salute for encouraging me to become a full-time writer.

Thanks also to Lovelace Cook for her author-to-author advisory efforts.

For taking this project from manuscript to finished book, thanks to Black Belt Press and the NewSouth Bookstore, and staffers Suzanne La Rosa, Randall Williams, Lisa Emerson, Jessala White, and Gabbi Emerson.

# Introduction — The Photographers

Almost all photographs in this book were taken by two persons—Paul Robertson and John Engelhardt Scott. In the text and captions, Robertson's images are from his estate and are credited as PR. Scott's images, labeled as ADAH, are from his collection that is maintained by the Alabama Department of Archives and History.

## PAUL ROBERTSON

One of the most popular Montgomery photographers in the latter half of the twentieth century, Paul Jene Robertson was born in Mattoon, Illinois (south of Champaign-Urbana), in 1925. His family was somewhat migratory; his father worked in several occupations, including as an interior decorator for a major department store in Chicago. Eventually the Robertsons ended up in Montgomery, where the patriarch took a job at the Victorian Furniture manufacturing company.

Paul's formal education ended after several months in the tenth grade. He became interested in photography and began what would become his lifelong occupation at veteran Stanley Paulger's photography studio, located on Court Square in downtown Montgomery.

Robertson joined the U.S. Navy at age seventeen, during World War II. Stationed in Hawaii for an extensive time, he served as a tail gunner on a PBY aircraft and as a machinist's mate. He later had a billeted assignment in Memphis, where he met and married Wylodene Belew. They would have two sons, Paul Jr. and David.

A family legend recounts that like a lot of World War II veterans, Paul was pondering what he was going to do for a job when he was processed out of the Navy in Memphis. He happened to spot the Woodard School of Photography in that city and decided to try that occupation, since he'd had a modicum of experience before the war with Stanley

Paulger in Montgomery. Paul's Woodward education was financed by the then-new G.I. Bill.

Returning to Montgomery in 1948, Paul worked with up-and-coming peers Laurens Pierce and Jay Leavell. Robertson and Pierce shot Montgomery's first television film footage in 1950, and Paul established his own business in 1951. Pierce would later be on the scene of historical events including the Freedom Riders' arrival in Montgomery in 1961 and the 1972 assassination attempt on Governor George Wallace in Maryland. Leavell became a noted Montgomery advertising executive.

Paul began his solo career by creating a no-frills, functional studio in his family's home on Plum Street in the Highland Park section of Montgomery. At one point, his advertising slogan was "Anything–Anytime–Anywhere."

In addition to developing a clientele for his portrait work, Paul photographed weddings and other social events and continued to do freelance news photography,

*Above: Paul Sr., Paul Jr., and David outside Dad 'N' Lad during the opening of Normandale's arcade in early 1957. Below: On occasion, Paul drafted family members as models to get an appropriate photo. That's Wylodene and their two boys window shopping at Normandale (PR).*

particularly for the local newspapers. *Montgomery Advertiser* city editor Joe Azbell relied on him for coverage of events, and society editor Esther "Go Peep" Mahoney—and later, Madera Spencer—counted on Paul's affable attitude when he photographed debutantes at formal balls. He was also a stringer for the Associated Press (paid per assignment). One of his most famous images was a photo of Martin Luther King Jr. being booked at the Montgomery Police Department, which was published in *Life* magazine more than once.

Paul became a legendary photographer in Montgomery, and served with various Montgomery civic organizations and charities.

The senior Robertson expanded his business to eventually include his sons and his grandson, David Jr. The multi-generation company was known as "Photography by the Robertsons" and operated in Montgomery for decades. Paul Sr. had reason to be proud of his family business. One of the buildings owned by the Robertsons eventually contained some forty file cabinets full of archival negatives. David thought the total number of negatives could have been as high as 300,000. And in his later days, Paul Sr. had no desire to sort through them.

Following Paul's death in 2020 at age ninety-five, his sons discovered a cache of undated and unlabeled negatives in several canvas bags. Among the assortment were dozens of images of the Normandale shopping center in south Montgomery, shown in various phases of construction or as completed units. Among them were numerous photos of Normandale business owners and shoppers, as well as special events, including the memorable 1957 visit of that year's Miss America, Marian McKnight of South Carolina.

Those photos generated positive memories for Paul Jr. and David. Research indicated

that Robertson's earliest Normandale image was of a preview sign being installed at the corner of Patton Avenue and Norman Bridge Road, probably taken in early 1954, as the shopping center's groundbreaking ceremony was held December 11, 1953.

## JOHN ENGELHARDT SCOTT

John Engelhardt Scott (1915–2000) was born in Montgomery, but early in his childhood his father, a civil engineer for L&N Railroad, moved the family to Louisville, Kentucky, where John grew up. Following high school, he attended the University of the South in Sewanee, Tennessee. His father was an avid amateur photographer, so the younger Scott was motivated towards the camera lens as well.

John moved to Chicago and designed window

*Photo by John Engelhardt Scott Jr. of Camp Callan searchlight pattern. (Courtesy of James Scott)*

displays for major department stores. He also met his future wife June Buckardt, a Chicago native.

John was drafted into the U.S. Army in June 1942. He went through Officer Candidate School and was stationed at locations across the country. June and John married that same year. Assisted by her in-laws, June moved to Montgomery during the war.

One of John's military assignments was as a photographer and public relations officer to a coastal watch company at Camp Callan, located near San Diego. One of his particularly creative photographs depicted searchlights at Camp Callan. The angle from which John took the image lined up the searchlight patterns to look like the Japanese "Rising Sun" flag. Later he joined the Signal Corps, setting up communications for George Patton's Third Army in Europe.

Following the end of the conflict, John returned to Montgomery and opened his photography business in 1946. June was active in her husband's business as office manager and critic. They raised two daughters, Elizabeth and Ann, and three sons, John III, William, and James.

John Scott retired after operating his photography enterprise for forty-five years. He was admired among his peers for innovative commercial photography, underlined by his methodical, efficient, business-like and perhaps even scientific approach to his assignments, particularly when photographing landmarks and buildings. Accordingly, he was popular among local architects. Alabama Department of Archives and History official (and daughter-in-law) Mary Jo Scott opined that he was more comfortable in those types of assignments.

John's diverse services included aerial photography, murals, portraits, catalogs, yearbooks and special events. The aerial images were challenging;

John would strap himself into the passenger seat of a small private airplane and hang out the open cabin door to get an optimum shot. He had business partners as well subordinate photographers as employees, but such associations often didn't last, most likely because of Scott's intense focus on integrity, quality and hard work.

Among the special events Scott photographed was a speech by Robert Kennedy in the Blue-Gray Room at the Whitley Hotel. A resulting photograph is a bit of a mystery. It is thought that the photo was taken in 1959, before Kennedy's brother John had been elected president and before RFK was U.S. attorney general (he looks younger in the photo to some viewers). Another veteran Alabama photographer, Tommy Giles, was an assistant to Governor John Patterson in that era, and he confirmed the location of the photo and notes that Patterson is standing at the lectern. Giles believes the occasion might have been an early campaign meeting among Alabama Democrats; he consulted with Patterson's son Albert for details.

"We believe that this was a private meeting of a small group," said Giles. "Maybe to raise funds for JFK and start a grassroots campaign. I *do* know that John was the first governor to endorse JFK. John made several trips to Washington and to Massachussetts to meet with JFK and his family about the race. I think the three men to RFK's left are members of Congress from Alabama. At this time we had nine members in Congress; later, we went to seven with them running state-wide."

*John Scott photo of Robert Kennedy (standing, second from left) in Montgomery, ca. 1959. Governor John Patterson is standing at the microphone at left. (ADAH)*

Patterson, Kennedy, and several other individuals pictured are wearing boutonnieres. "John wore a boutonniere every day," Giles said of the Alabama governor. "I used to pin it on."

Interestingly, the large murals seen in the background in that facility were also Scott images.

John Scott developed a relationship with the Alabama Department of Archives and History (ADAH) that lasted for decades, and he also taught photography classes at Huntingdon College in his later years. When he died in 2000, it wasn't surprising that the ADAH was the recipient of his meticulously catalogued collection of more than 78,000 images.

PAUL ROBERTSON, JOHN ENGELHARDT Scott Jr., and Tommy Giles were active members of the Montgomery Professional Photographers' Association; Scott was the organization's first president, and Giles was its second. All three men won numerous awards from national photographic organizations. They forged a decades-long friendship based on mutual respect and dedication to their craft. Paul Robertson Jr. was a pallbearer at John's funeral.

# The Golden Age
## of Normandale

*Above, developer Aaron Aronov, 1954—ADAH. Inset at top, his father, Jake Aronov, in 1928.*

# 1

# The (Shopping) City Upon a Hillock

Normandale Shopping City was indeed built atop a small hill, on twenty-two and a half acres near the new Southern By-Pass in south Montgomery. And in those days, the By-Pass *really was* a bypass.

What's more, the shopping center's early advocates, such as Ed Dombrowski, Bill Denson, and Meredith Harrell (in that order), would have you think that Normandale was Xanadu, Camelot, and the Emerald City rolled into one.

The visionary behind the construction of the legendary Alabama retail lodestone was local real estate developer Aaron Aronov, the son of Jake Aronov, a Ukrainian immigrant. Aaron was born in Montgomery in 1919. He attended the University of Alabama in Tuscaloosa for two years before his father's illness compelled his return to Montgomery, where he worked in his family's business, Jake Aronov Auto Parts & Tire Company. Jake died at age forty-nine in October 1943.

Aaron's younger son Owen said, "My father didn't really enjoy working in the automobile tire and accessory business. He remembered that when he was growing up, his father would build three or four houses a year, as a type of hobby that he really enjoyed. His family would move into a house while he built another one, and then they'd move into the new one and sell the previous one."

Aaron's life partner was Marjorie Schoenbaum, who was born in Alexander City, Alabama, where her father ran a general mercantile store. To describe the Aronovs' mid-1940s courtship as a whirlwind romance is an understatement—according to Owen, his parents had dated for three weeks when they became engaged. Three weeks after the engagement was announced, they married, on September 2, 1945, at the Jefferson Davis Hotel in downtown Montgomery. The resulting family would include sons Jake and Owen and a daughter, Teri.

Aaron's interest in residential housing and commercial construction steadily grew. "He was intrigued with taking a vacant piece of land and using your imagination to build something on it," said Owen. "He watched concrete being poured, sheetrock being installed, and electricians working. He decided to go out on his own in the real estate business."

ARONOV REALTY WAS FOUNDED in 1952 and had already been establishing residential areas in Montgomery when Aaron's concept of what would become Normandale Shopping City evolved. Not long after Aaron's company was established, he optioned a large tract of land in south Montgomery that in the early 1800s had been a plantation owned by the Mastin family. The Mastins' elegant mansion was called Fairview, for which a long thoroughfare in south Montgomery eventually was named.

The "Norman" part of the area's name was the

surname of pioneers Job and Rebecca Norman, who had settled in the area of what later became Harrison Elementary School, on the Southern By-Pass near the intersection of Norman Bridge Road. The Normans had twelve children, and the family's lands extended south to Catoma Creek.

"Normandale" was the name of Aronov's new residential subdivision before it was assigned to the shopping center. Owen recalled how the changes in national residential trends influenced his father's land acquisition in the early 1950s. "The 'suburbanization' of America was taking place. People were moving into homes further from downtown, which was the essence of why Normandale Shopping Center was built. My father had a vision that people would appreciate being able to do their everyday shopping in close proximity to their homes, which was a sensible concept to him."

Aaron hired a land planner from Texas and began endeavoring to build a community of some four hundred homes on two hundred-plus acres. "Part of that land was designated (as having) a commercial configuration," said Owen, "and it was called a 'shopping center' in the plans. Nobody had heard that term before." Accordingly, Aaron Aronov's dream of a gigantic, one-of-a-kind, all-encompassing retail center was only one part of the "Normandale" concept.

FINANCIERS AT MONTGOMERY banks admired Aronov's moxie, but balked at taking shoppers away from downtown, which in the middle of the twentieth century was the hub of retail activity in "The Cradle of the Confederacy." Since the 1820s, Montgomery's banks, theaters, department stores, fashion shops, and the post office had filled out the historic downtown nestled in a bend in the Alabama River. The state capitol and related functions and offices moved to the city in the late 1840s, and the Confederacy was briefly headquartered there in 1861.

Unable to get local financing for his well-planned initiative and dream, Aaron persevered. A business acquaintance advised him to seek financing in Chicago, where big city bankers had more experience with this new "shopping center" concept.

"That's where he got his loan," Owen said, "resulting in the construction of Normandale Shopping Center, which became extraordinarily successful."

Montgomery already had a primeval, nondescript shopping center known as Cloverland, located on South Court Street near Bellingrath School. It was relatively small, boxy, and mundane, and its "anchor unit" was a grocery store. Normandale was to be located a few blocks east of Cloverland, which would be dwarfed by the size and aesthetics of Aronov's ambitious project.

*Cloverland Shopping Center—ADAH.*

*State Coliseum (today, Garrett Coliseum)—ADAH.*

When Aronov purchased it for the new shopping center, the acreage at the intersection of Norman Bridge Road and Patton Avenue was a hay field. Legend has it that Aronov would later stand in that hay field and shake hands with Birmingham retail officials to secure the new center's anchor store.

THE ARCHITECTURAL FIRM FOR the massive undertaking was Sherlock, Smith & Adams of Montgomery. The renowned firm had recently executed a design by Betty Robison, the first female architecture graduate of Auburn University, for the new Alabama State Coliseum, which had been constructed in the northeast area of the city near Gunter Air Force Base. The first large event staged at the Coliseum (renamed Garrett Coliseum in 1963 in honor of the state agriculture commissioner) was a Hank Williams "homecoming" concert in July 1951. Performers included Hank Snow, the Carter Family, and an up-and-coming guitarist named Chet Atkins. One ad promoting the upcoming event said it would be "The Greatest Hillbilly Show Ever in Montgomery!"

To some observers, the Coliseum's swooping Mid-Century Modern lines resembled a giant turtle, but the imposing building's interior and exterior designs were functional. Sherlock, Smith & Adams sought to blend the same excitement and practical innovation in the design of Normandale Shopping Center, and more than one intriguing aspect of architectural styles would be interpolated into construction of the facility. A later newspaper article named the Copeland, Novak and Associates company of New York City as associate architects.

THE PLANNED RETAIL LINEUP for the original Normandale Shopping Center was meant to offer a one-stop shopping experience. A large department store would be the anchor unit, supported ideally by women's, men's, and children's clothing stores, as well as shoe, furniture, eyeglass, luggage, flower, toy, candy, hardware, fabric, auto parts, and photography supply stores, as well as a bakery, pharmacy, grocery, and a "five-and-dime" variety store. "Service" businesses would include a beauty shop, a barber shop, a bank, a shoe repair/leather goods store, a laundromat, a dry cleaners, and doctors' and dentists' offices.

Other facets of the overall plan included plenty of free parking (downtown Montgomery had parking meters), and a policy that all stores would be open at the same hours.

Plenty of promotions would attract customers.

The tenants could participate in composite advertising, which would be at least a full page in the local newspaper.

By the time Aronov's quest for local financing was denied, he had already held commitments for a department store and a grocery store. Loveman's, headquartered in Birmingham, was interested in expanding and quickly came to terms with Aronov to become Normandale's anchor department store. The grocery store anchor would be Kwik Chek, a Montgomery-based chain under the aegis of another legendary Montgomery businessman, Tine Davis of the Winn-Dixie grocery empire.

Aronov Realty Company would become the agent for a new company, the Normandale Development Corporation, that would oversee the shopping center's construction and the establishment of its retail stores.

Loveman's was announced as Normandale Shopping Center's central store by Joe Azbell, city editor of the *Montgomery Advertiser*, on the front page of the morning newspaper's April 19, 1953, issue. Citing Loveman's President O. W. Shanbacher as a source, Azbell noted that Loveman's would be an air-conditioned two-story building of eighty thousand square feet. Its *moving stairs* between floors would be the first escalators installed in a retail establishment in central Alabama, if not in the entire state.

Another story on the same page was the official announcement of the coming shopping center *in toto*. Aaron Aronov stated that the planning had included trips to Dallas, High Point (North Carolina), Tulsa, Atlanta, Los Angeles, Birmingham, New Orleans,

Chicago, and other cities to examine other new shopping centers. He declared that Normandale officials had been "swamped with scores of applications" from potential stores. He estimated that the shopping center would open in the spring of 1954.

Initial promotion in the spring of 1953 included a "Live in Normandale" ad that hyped the residential subdivision's attributes, including the proximity of schools, churches, and municipal bus service. The ad also displayed a line drawing of the coming Loveman's store.

FOR WHATEVER REASONS, CONSTRUCTION started later than expected, as the groundbreaking ceremony wasn't held until December 11, 1953. In his "City Limits" newspaper column two days later, Joe Azbell recounted how a spectator at the groundbreaking asked where Loveman's would be located in the hay field, to which an official of the Normandale Development Corporation quipped, "You're standing next to the hosiery counter right now." A listing in the December 31, 1953, *Montgomery Advertiser* ranked the announcement of the coming shopping center as the paper's sixth most significant news story of the year.

A "coming soon" sign displaying an illustration of the Loveman's anchor store was erected at the intersection of Norman Bridge Road and Patton Avenue. A temporary fence around part of the construction added to the mystery and mystique of the project.

"It was common knowledge that [the Aronov company] was building a shopping center out there," said Rubin Franco, a second-generation owner of Franco Distributing Company, which

**Joe Azbell**

# LIVE IN *Normandale*

## Montgomery's Finest Home Development
## NO EXTRA COST!

All improvements are included in the original land cost
- Gas • Water • Paving •Curb Gutters

All Have Been Included

### NO EXTRA ASSESSMENTS

The Southern section has always been Montgomery's best real estate value for homes. Normandale restrictions and location offer the soundest home sites and values in the city. Normandale is designed for the family who wants to own their own home.

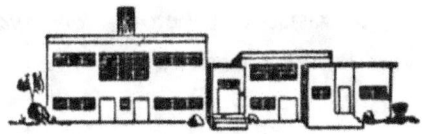

Served by
## 2 MAIN BUS LINES

Normandale is only six to ten minutes from downtown Montgomery.

### CLOSE TO SCHOOLS
One block from the new grade school, six blocks from Junior High and within walking distance of Sidney Lanier High.

### FINE CHURCHES NEARBY
Some of Montgomery's finest Churches are planned for Normandale.

### PROTECTED PROPERTY
You will be protected in Normandale, because your property is restricted. Minimum size home requirement 1,250 square feet of living space. Your home will be a safer investment because of these restrictions.

### HIGH AND DRY
The highest land in Cloverdale with excellent drainage over-looking this beautiful vista of surrounding countryside and gently curving streets.

## SHOPPING CENTER

. . . In the process of development. One of the most beautifully planned shopping centers in the South, containing one of Alabama's finest department stores, complete men's shop, novelty stores, in addition, of course to super market and drug centers. No parking meters, plenty of free parking space—so located to enhance the value of all Normandale.

PR

On this site — watch it !
*Loveman's* —OF ALABAMA WILL OPEN A NEW MONTGOMERY DEPARTMENT STORE - WITH THE FINEST SELECTIONS OF MERCHANDISE FOR THE HOME & THE ENTIRE FAMILY

*Work in progress: This mid-February 1954 photo shows the west end of the original Normandale front line retail store lineup. Lee's Cut-Rate Drugs became the original tenant here—ADAH.*

had been founded in 1928 by his father. The Francos' enterprise set up and maintained candy and cigarette vending machines around the Capital City. Jukeboxes were another facet of the business, and the company was also interested in the placement of "kiddie rides" and perhaps vending machines at Normandale.

In May 1954, an advertising campaign designated the house at 3568 Berkley Drive as "the Normandale Home." To promote the under-construction shopping center, the residence was completely furnished and decorated by Loveman's. Some sixty additional homes and lots in the Normandale subdivision would be developed at the same time the gigantic retail complex was being built. However, it wasn't long before *Normandale* as a solitary word became mostly a reference to the shopping center.

Making up time for the delayed groundbreaking, construction proceeded at a faster-than-anticipated pace. One of the primary reasons—and something in which Aaron Aronov took great pride—was the almost-exclusive use of Montgomery companies in building the shopping center.

Jehle Brothers Construction Company was named as the contractor for the immense project. By the shopping center's grand opening, up to a hundred homes in Normandale Estates had also been built by the contractor, which had recently diversified into other building styles. Jehle Brothers proved itself up to the challenge of Normandale Shopping Center. An estimated two hundred-plus construction workers were on-site daily. The contractor also utilized twenty sub-contractors.

It was thought that clearing the land would take up to two months, but using a reported half million dollars' worth of equipment, the Vandigriff Construction Co. accomplished the task in ten days.

Loveman's was centered between two lines of smaller stores and shops

for the first time ... see the home
All Montgomery is waiting to see

The Normandale Home Is Located At 3568 Berkley Drive

*Top, the front parking area has designated lanes and light poles in place prior to paving—PR; Middle, as the parking lot takes shape, three store signs on the northeast line are already up, over areas that are still under construction—PR; Bottom, first configuration of Normandale Shopping Center—ADAH.*

located on northeast and west-facing sections of the original configuration. Seen from the air, the layout of the entire shopping center resembled a question mark.

CUSTOMERS WOULD STROLL THROUGH Normandale on wide sidewalks under a canopy roof that was ten feet high and fifteen feet wide to block the rain. Benches were placed on the sidewalks at strategic locations, and light instrumental music was piped through speakers on the ceilings. The sound system could also be a public address system/intercom.

White neon lighting with each store's name was installed on the parapet wall above the canopy, and small, simple signs with each business's name were suspended from the ceiling of the walkway in front of each store. Most of the store names on the parapet included company logo names or trademarks—the "check mark" for Kwik Chek grocery, the block letters and "hurricane S" seen in the original logo for Mel's Photo Shop, etc. An exception to the store name colors was F. W. Woolworth, a huge national variety store chain. The Woolworth's store in Normandale was originally located next to the Kwik Chek, and the retailer was allowed to display its name in the company's standard red block letters.

There would be no flashiness or glitz in window displays; blinking lights and colored neon were not allowed.

As the anchor unit, Loveman's drew a shopper's attention with an imposing façade in the International style of architectural design—clean straight lines, often with exposed/open spaces underneath. Supported by round columns, a large display area on the second floor overhung the sidewalk. The mostly marble exterior featured two huge windows to display merchandise (usually seasonal), with an exception made for the right-facing window during the Christmas season. The underside of the second-floor extension lined up smoothly with the walkway on the first floor, and three large display windows on the ground floor under the extension proffered fashionable clothing (usually displayed on mannequins) and other wares.

Like the F. W. Woolworth store, Loveman's also had a minor exemption regarding the lighting policy, with back lighting installed behind the store name to provide a silhouette effect.

THE FACT THAT ALL stores would be air-conditioned generated enormous publicity. Air-conditioning—including window-mounted units for homes, as sold by more than one Normandale store—was still a new-fangled luxury for many consumers.

Another highly publicized facet of Normandale's construction was the extensive use of glass—some

*Canopied walkways at Normandale featured lighting and music speakers installed overhead. Loveman's International-style façade is also seen in this view from the west side—ADAH.*

*Nighttime image of the Kwik Chek grocery emphasizes the lines of its façade's unique Mid-Century Modern architectural style.—ADAH*

1,300 linear feet of quarter-inch Pittsburgh Plate glass, according to a press release. Of that, Loveman's utilized a disproportionate amount in its gigantic front windows on the second floor and the three display windows on the first floor. And glass figured prominently into the Kwik Chek design. Sections of glass on the front of the grocery formed a see-through façade that stretched from the floor to the roof, and each piece at the top end had to be custom-cut to fit the curvature.

Kwik Chek's arched roof hinted at a Mid-Century Modern style, and many observers probably wondered if it was at least partially inspired by the new State Coliseum on the other side of town. The sides of the curved canopy atop the Kwik Chek actually tapered inwards, a feature that was difficult to discern from the front of the building. Aerial photos revealed that from overhead the silhouette of the unusual roof had a trapezoid shape. Close observation from the side revealed that the roofline tapered downward from front to rear; i.e., the glass front edge was taller than the rear edge. According to a Montgomery architect who had frequented Normandale as a youngster, such a style "... meant that every structural span component was different and individual, if spanning across."

Since the aesthetics of the Kwik Chek roof vaguely alluded to a band shell, perhaps it wasn't surprising that a rumor circulated that the space occupied by the grocery store was originally supposed to have been a theater.

*Penn Fruit, a chain of grocery stores based in Philadelphia, built several stores in the 1950s that had a similar look, like this one in Allentown, Pennsylvania—Wikimedia Commons.*

NUMEROUS RETAILERS IN DOWNTOWN Montgomery planned on expanding to Normandale. Like the contractors that built Normandale, its list of retail stores was primarily of local and regional businesses. Retailers like Montgomery Shoe Factory ran small "preview" newspaper ads to notify customers about their upcoming new store in south Montgomery.

To some, a hardware store lined up with numerous clothing stores and a grocery store may have seemed a bit awkward, but the inclusion of Parker-Sledge Hardware—right in front—validated Normandale's all-in-one concept.

ED DOMBROWSKI, A COMBAT veteran of World War II, was hired as the general manager of Normandale. The Erie, Pennsylvania, native had been a

*Ed Dombrowski—ADAH.*

B-25 bombardier in Europe and was shot down but escaped from his German captors. He slowly and carefully worked his way back to Allied lines and discovered the U.S. Army Air Forces had declared him dead. He was sent back to the United States and happened to arrive at his home in Erie while his family was attending *his* memorial service.

Dombrowski's responsibilities with Normandale included maintaining appropriate relations with tenants, promotions, media relations (including press releases—advertisements in a narrative format) and monitoring the appearance and cleanliness of the facility.

It had been estimated that the overall construction of the Normandale Shopping Center would take up to two years to complete. Jehle Brothers Construction Co. and its subcontractors did the job in about nine months.

The grand opening of Normandale Shopping Center was scheduled for Friday, September 10, 1954. The day before, the pending event was the lead story on Page One of the *Montgomery Advertiser,* under Joe Azbell's byline. Azbell's "City Limits" column in the same issue was also devoted exclusively to the opening of Normandale and was effusive in its praise for the project's progenitors. Normandale's grand opening was also cited on Page One of Montgomery's evening newspaper, the *Alabama Journal,* but its lead story was about an earthquake that had killed hundreds of people in Algeria.

The September 9 editions of the *Advertiser* and the *Journal* contained a huge special advertising section with succinct and informative monographs profiling the businesses and individuals that had developed and built the facility, as well as articles and profiles of merchants and their businesses.

THE GRAND OPENING CEREMONY on September 10 was highlighted by a ribbon cutting. The scissors

*Loveman's employees unpack mannequins on September 7, 1954—three days before the grand opening—ADAH.*

were manipulated by Jason Smith, age ninety-two, who was thought to be one of the oldest citizens of Montgomery. Mayor W. A. "Tacky" Gayle made what was termed as "the official address" at the event.

Among the attendees at the grand opening was John Smith, an Atlanta real estate developer with an idea for a shopping center that would be called Lenox Square. "He introduced himself to my father," said Owen, "and said that he was trying to develop a similar idea in a much larger setting. They became dear friends, and would chat with each other frequently, trading ideas. Some years later, my father was the president of the International Council of Shopping Centers, and after my father's tenure, John Smith became president. The

developers would learn from each other." Lenox Square opened in 1959.

Riding the newfangled escalators in Loveman's was an exciting but sometimes awkward experience for many customers, some of whom didn't know how to coordinate placing their feet onto what were essentially stair steps that were in motion. Montgomery firemen were temporarily stationed by the escalators on both floors to assist any customer who might literally step into trouble.

The official full page ad for the grand opening listed merchants in alphabetical order and touted "A Few of the Features That Await You at Normandale." The type is small but the list can be read in the reproduced ad on page 14.

## Here Are A Few Of The Features That Await You At Normandale

- Every Possible Type Merchandise
- Spacious Free Paved Parking Area. Accommodations for 3,500 Cars
- Every Store Completely Air Conditioned
- Montgomery's First Escalators
- Elevator Service
- Covered Walkways To Protect You From Sun and Rain
- Redwod Benches
- Music Under Canopy
- Doctors' Building
- Cafeteria (soon)
- Convenient Lounge
- White and Colored Restrooms

# NORMANDALE

## Normandale Stores Invite You To The Grand Opening

- CLAY CRUMPTON LAUNDROMAT
  Automatic Laundry
- CAPITOL CLOTHING STORE
  Men's Clothing & Furnishings
- CITY FLORAL CO.
  Flowers and Plants
- DOCTORS' BLDG.
  10 Doctors
- DeSHIELDS-LARSON SHOE STORE
  Shoes for the Family
- DARBY & SONS
  Dry Cleaners & Launderers
- ROSLYN EAGLE
  Furniture and Gifts
- ELLIS OPTICAL CO.
  Optician
- FRANCIS CAFETERIA
  Cafeteria
- FLACK'S
  Ladies' Clothing
- LOU HERMAN'S
  Children's Clothing
- HARRELSON BARBER SHOP
  Barber Shop
- KWIK CHEK
  Super Market
- LEE'S
  Self-Service Drugs
- LOVEMAN'S
  Department Store
- LIGER'S BAKERY
  Bakery
- LOUISE BEAUTY SHOP
  Beauty Shop
- MONTGOMERY SHOE FACTORY
  Shoe Repairing & Leather Goods
- MEL'S PHOTO SHOP
  Photographic Equipment & Supplies
- NORMANDALE DELICATESSEN
  Delicatessen
- PARKER SLEDGE HARDWARE
  Hardware
- PAULINE WILKINS
  Ladies' Sportswear
- SAUL'S SHOE STORE
  Family Shoe Store
- TOWN & COUNTRY
  Ladies' Sportswear
- TOYLAND
  Toys
- WRIGHT'S INTERIORS
  Fabrics and Draperies
- WOOLWORTH
  Variety Store

# OPENS FRIDAY AT 10:00 A.M.

## WELCOME TO THE SOUTH'S LARGEST SHOPPING CENTER

For almost two years you've been reading and hearing about Normandale, watching its buildings rise and its spacious park-like environs take shape. Now it is ready to open — the largest and finest shopping center ever built in the South — a complete shopping town. There is so much to tell you about it, but we think the best way to find out all about its wonder-ful features is for you to visit Normandale during this grand opening. Loveman's and Normandale's other 28 shops and stores invite you most cordially to see what has been planned and built for your shopping needs, for your comfort and for your service and pleasure at Normandale. Welcome to Normandale's opening Friday at 10 a.m.

### Free Buses to Normandale

EXPRESS BUSES will leave Court Square every fifteen minutes—commencing at 9:30 a.m. and every fifteen minutes thereafter throughout the day and early evening. Express buses will return to Court Square every fifteen minutes from Normandale. The buses will be labeled NORMANDALE EXPRESS. THIS SERVICE WILL COMMENCE FRIDAY MORNING—AND CONTINUE ALL DAY SATURDAY AND MONDAY. Thereafter there will be convenient Montgomery City Line schedules to Normandale. Remember, Friday, Saturday and Monday — free express buses to Normandale every fifteen minutes from Court Square for your convenience during our grand opening.

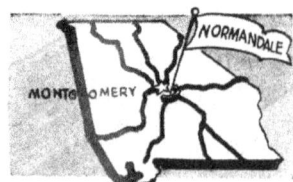

### Conveniently Located To Serve a Half Million People in Area

Normandale is conveniently located to serve Montgomery and all of Central and South Alabama. It is only a short distance to Normandale from all highways leading into Montgomery. Located just off Norman Bridge Road (Alabama Highway 9 south) eight blocks south of Fairview Avenue, it is conveniently located for those who live outside Montgomery to drive directly to Normandale without going through downtown traffic. It will make shopping in Montgomery easier than ever before for an estimated half a million people live within one to two hours driving time to Alabama's Capital City. If you live south, west, east or north of Montgomery—drive directly to Normandale for your complete shopping needs.

### The Biggest Shoppers' Parking Lot in Alabama at Normandale

There are acres of paved, clearly marked parking spaces surrounding Normandale — all free. These are angled parking spaces making it easy to get in and out with your car. It is only a few short steps to the covered walkway leading to our 28 shops and stores.

We suggest that you notice the numbered parking aisle where you leave your car and make a note of it so that it will be easy to find your car on your return. Just make a quick note of your parking aisle and you can quickly return to your car when you are ready to leave. Remember, no meters . . . no time limit!

REGULAR STORE HOURS FOR MOST NORMANDALE STORES: MONDAY, THURSDAY AND FRIDAY — 10:00 A.M. TO 9:00 P.M.
TUESDAY, WEDNESDAY AND SATURDAY 10:00 A.M. TO 5:45 P.M.; THIS FRIDAY & SATURDAY HOURS 10:00 A.M. TO 9:00 P.M.

*Above: Full parking lot on opening day, September 10, 1954. Right: The view from the Loveman's upstairs display window. Both, ADAH.*

*Above: Ribbon cutting participants included nonagenarian Jason Smith (light suit, bow tie). Montgomery Mayor W. A. "Tacky" Gayle is seated to Smith's right in the dark suit.—Albert Kraus Collection/Tommy Giles Photographic Services. Right: A clown added to the celebratory mood in front of DeShields-Larson Shoes—ADAH. Below right: Window shopping at Toyland—Albert Kraus Collection/Tommy Giles Photographic Services. Below: The ice cream station in Lee's Cut-Rate Drugs was located near the front of the store and quickly became popular among Normandale shoppers—ADAH.*

THE NORMANDALE MERCHANTS' ASSOCIATION was created in time for the grand opening, with the convivial Dave Larson of DeShields-Larson Shoes serving as its first president. Other officers included vice-president Leo Chrietzberg, treasurer Bernice Basch, and secretary Mel Price. Executive committee members included Harry Cohn, R. L. Crouch, and Ralph Phillips.

The Francis Cafeteria wasn't ready for business by the grand opening and would open in November; the Doctors' Building above the Francis Cafeteria also wouldn't be fully occupied until then.

*From left, front: Dave Larson, Leo Chrietzberg; back, Ed Dombrowski, Bernice Basch, Mel Price—Newspapers.com.*

Nevertheless, a photo caption trumpeted "Normandale is now a complete city within a city!" in the grand opening special advertising section of the local newspapers. "Ready to greet and serve the public—a beautiful monument to the business and residential life of Montgomery."

Another ad proclaimed Normandale to be "The largest, most modern air-conditioned shopping center in the entire South!"

Normandale's standard shopping hours were 10 a.m.–9 p.m. on Mondays, Thursdays and Fridays, and 10 a.m.–5:45 p.m. on Tuesdays, Wednesdays and Saturdays. The shopping center was closed on Sundays.

While the advance advertising had boasted that Normandale had 3,500 free paved parking spaces, that number was eventually downsized to 3,001. And the

*Top: Window-shoppers outside Toyland on Grand Opening Day. Above: Customers wait outside Loveman's for the doors to open. Note the gentleman's dapper two-tone shoes. Both—ADAH.*

grand opening ad had referred to the facility as simply "Normandale," not "Normandale Shopping Center."

Aaron Aronov was thirty-four when Normandale Shopping Center opened in September 1954. He was already an active supporter of local nonprofit organizations and charities, including the YMCA, and had also served as chairman of the 1949 March of Dimes campaign. Over the coming years, his real estate development business would flourish, building shopping centers and residential subdivisions in numerous states.

~

*Some fifteen months after the opening of Normandale, Joe Azbell would passively assist in the birth of the Montgomery Bus Boycott.*

*Seamstress Rosa Parks had been arrested on a Montgomery City Lines municipal bus on December 1, 1955, for refusing to surrender her seat to a white passenger. Activists in the city's black community were planning a bus boycott as a protest, but they were having trouble getting the word out.*

*"Negro news" was usually located fairly deep within the pages of the* Montgomery Advertiser *and the* Alabama Journal, *but Azbell decided to place a news story titled*

*"Negro Groups Ready Boycott of City Lines" on the front page of the December 4 edition of the* Advertiser.

*It was later acknowledged by Martin Luther King Jr. and other civil rights activists that Azbell's decision was one of the strongest and most beneficial actions that generated initial interest in the bus boycott.*

# 2

# The Grand Ole Opry Comes to Town

To say that Normandale Shopping Center hit the ground running with promotional events is an understatement. A mere ten days after its grand opening, Normandale held an outdoor concert as part of a two-day Hank Williams Memorial event (September 20–21, 1954), sponsored by the Alcazar Shrine Temple.

Governor Gordon Persons had declared September 21 as "Hank Williams Day" in Alabama, and a plethora of Grand Ole Opry stars had agreed to travel to Montgomery to participate in events such as the laying of a wreath at Williams's grave and a visit to a military hospital at Maxwell Air Force Base. The day would conclude with a huge concert at Cramton Bowl, home of the Blue-Gray college all-star football game and home field for Sidney Lanier High School (Williams had attended Lanier but did not graduate). Some of the Nashville stars had also attended Williams's funeral in Montgomery on January 4, 1953.

The 1954 memorial celebration was actually to begin on September 20, with three dances simultaneously staged at Fort Dixie Graves Armory, the Shrine Temple, and the Montgomery City Auditorium. All three were to begin at 7:45.

In a shrewd marketing ploy, Ed Dombrowski staged a free "tribute to Hank Williams, his mother and his family," starting at 6 p.m. in the Normandale parking lot. Dombrowski figured that by ending the Normandale show at 6:45, the Hank Williams fans in attendance would have an hour to get to one of the three dances later the same evening.

Up-and-coming country singer Ferlin Husky was booked to perform on Normandale's temporary

# TOMORROW NIGHT - 6 To 6:45
## NORMANDALE PAYS TRIBUTE TO THE LATE, GREAT MONTGOMERIAN, HANK WILLIAMS

From our elevated stage, tomorrow (Monday) night, 6 to 6:45, Normandale is happy to play host to Mrs. Lillian Williams Stone (Hank's mother), Audrey Williams and children, together with a large number of Hank Williams' friends who loved him and worked with him. Normandale is happy to be able to take part in the observance of Hank Williams' Day and cordially invite you to come out and help us pay tribute to Hank Williams, his mother and his family.

## Be Our Guest, All Free, Monday Night, 6 to 6:45; Come See These Famous Folk Artists and Stars In Person

★ Mrs. Lillian Williams Stone (Hank's Mother)

Audrey Williams and Children

★ Jimmie Davis
★ Hank Snow
★ Ernest Tubb

★ Chelette Sisters
★ R. D. Hendon
★ Ray Price

★ Pee Wee King
★ Jim Reeves

## PLUS SCORES OF OTHERS

### Music by: FERLIN HUSKEY and the DRIFTING COWBOYS (Hank's Old Band)

stage (a flatbed trailer), as was Williams's former band, the Drifting Cowboys.

The promotion of the memorial concert at Normandale was part of a full-page ad that thanked "Montgomery and All Alabama" for the reception to the grand opening of the shopping center. Scheduled attendees included Lillie Williams Stone (Hank's mother), Audrey Williams (Hank's former wife) and children, Jimmie Davis, Hank Snow, Ernest Tubb, the Chelette Sisters, R. D. Hendon, Pee Wee King, Ray Price, and Jim Reeves. The ad overstepped when its text promised ". . . Scores of Others."

At the Monday evening show, local gospel singer Leaborn Eads introduced Mayor W. A. Gayle and Shrine Potentate Joe Hedrick. Mrs. Stone was presented with a chest of sterling silver and a portrait of her son, unveiled by state senator Vaughan

Hill Robison. Audrey Williams and Hank's sister Irene received bouquets and corsages. Some media reports erroneously referred to Audrey Williams as Hank's widow.

Most of the celebrity musicians cited in the Normandale ad were expected to make just an appearance to publicize the three dances later that evening as well as the upcoming concert at Cramton Bowl the next night. However, several Nashville stars, including Snow, Davis, King, and Tubb reportedly sat in with the performers at the Normandale show.

Mayor Gayle estimated the Normandale crowd at ten thousand persons, which may have been a stretch, but the attendance was indeed impressive. The opportunity to participate in a city-wide initiative had proven to be a huge publicity boost for the new shopping center.

# 3

# Homecoming for a World Series Hero

Just two and a half weeks after the Hank Williams extravaganza, Ed Dombrowski and his Normandale associates took part in another highly publicized salute to another local hero. This honoree was still alive, and he had just completed a memorable performance in the world of professional sports.

Major league pinch hitter and outfielder James Lamar "Dusty" Rhodes of the New York Giants was originally from an unincorporated spot-in-the-road community called Mathews, Alabama, located in southeast Montgomery County. He'd had a mediocre baseball career in the minor leagues and with the New York Giants, who had acquired him in 1952.

But Rhodes's star went supernova in the 1954 World Series.

The favored Cleveland Indians had won 111 games during the regular season (a record for the American League). However, Dusty's bat would turn out to be a key factor for the Giants in the post-season classic.

The first game of the '54 Series is legendary because of "The Catch"—Willie Mays's over-the-shoulder snag of a long, hard shot by the Indians' Vic Wertz in the eighth inning is one of the most iconic moments in the history of Major League Baseball. And the Giants took an extra-inning victory in that game when Rhodes, pinch-hitting for outfielder Monte Irvin and facing future Hall of Fame pitcher Bob Lemon, clouted a three-run homer in the tenth inning for a 5–2 win.

Rhodes came through in the second game as well, with an RBI single in the fifth inning and a solo home run in the seventh

*Left: The Rhodes family arrives at the Montgomery airport, courtesy of a ride in Winton Blount's private plane—ADAH. Below: Presentation of gifts to the Rhodes family by Dave Larson, monitored by Walter Bamberg (light suit)—ADAH.*

to nail down a 3–1 triumph.

A two-run single in the third inning was Dusty's contribution to a third win by a score of 6–2. He wasn't used in the fourth and final game. Rhodes had garnered four hits and seven RBIs in the seven times he batted in the World Series.

The 1954 Fall Classic marked the first time the Giants had ever swept a World Series, and it was also the first time the Indians had ever lost a Series in four straight games.

It probably wasn't a surprise that the subsequent acclamation for Rhodes's performance in

# SATURDAY IS DUSTY RHODES DAY IN NORMANDALE

## Come On Out and Meet Dusty, Saturday, 11 A.M.

the World Series included the city of Montgomery pronouncing the slugger to be a native son, and a "hometown" celebration was quickly planned. The event was sponsored by the Montgomery Chamber of Commerce, the Downtown Merchants' Association, and the new Normandale Merchants' Association.

Accompanied by his wife Mae and his two young sons, Dusty Jr. and Ronnie, Rhodes flew into Montgomery's airport, Dannelly Field, on Friday afternoon, October 8. He participated in a press conference and was introduced at the Lanier–Ramsay (Birmingham) football game that evening.

Saturday saw a downtown parade and welcoming ceremony, followed by a similar event at Normandale. Rhodes and his family were presented with numerous gifts, including a new Mercury automobile.

Dave Larson officiated at Rhodes's appearance in front of Loveman's at Normandale, and up-and-coming local reporter Walter Bamberg was on hand with a microphone to cover the event as a live broadcast for WCOV-TV and Radio.

Following the events, Dusty and his family stayed in Montgomery for several days to visit with old friends. He had negotiated an endorsement deal with Ben R. Goltsman & Company, a local wholesale wine distributor, so while he was in the Capital City, he made an appointment with Paul Robertson for a new publicity photo in his Giants uniform. The photo session took place in the photographer's "studio" at his Plum Street residence. Paul's son David, then seven years old, wandered in and had an impromptu photo taken with the recent World Series hero. "I'm not sure I was old enough to know who Dusty Rhodes was or what he'd done," David recalled with a chuckle.

Rhodes would play with the Giants for several more years, but the 1954 World Series marked the pinnacle of his pro baseball career.

WCOV-TV (Channel 20, a CBS affiliate) and Walter Bamberg would ultimately be involved with numerous collaborations and promotions with Normandale. Channel 20 was Montgomery's first television station, having gone on the air in 1953. Bamberg, a Korean War veteran, was an early hire who worked his way into the local operations of the new video media business. The Normandale merchants also worked with WSFA-TV (Channel 12, an NBC affiliate), which went on the air in late 1954.

*Rhodes with David Robertson—PR.*

*Circus Acts Visit Normandale*
*Above, children and parents were delighted as clowns entertained a large crowd of shoppers. Below, pachyderms paraded in front of Loveman's. Both photos are from the Aronov Realty Company archives.*

# 4

# Further Mid-Fifties Growth

Within a month, Normandale's grand opening, participation in the Hank Williams Memorial commemoration, and the Dusty Rhodes homecoming had established the shopping center as a huge and competitive participant in the retail environment of central Alabama. The impressive promotional events were enthusiastically embraced by the Normandale Merchants' Association and the general public. Eager customers speculated about what other unique presentations might be in the offing.

In an immediate sign of cooperation, composite newspaper ads for multiple Normandale stores began appearing in late September (see page 23). October brought a week-long display inside Loveman's of a new Ford model, the sporty 1955 Thunderbird, in a collaboration with Al Means Ford, the local dealership. Thunderbirds were also displayed at other Loveman's stores in the state.

Then there was the October 27 visit to Normandale by clowns and elephants from the Hamid-Morton Circus, touted as the "World's Largest Indoor Circus." The Montgomery Junior Chamber of Commerce ("Jaycees") was sponsoring the three-ring circus at the Alabama Agricultural Coliseum, and Ed Dombrowski took his cue from September's successful Hank Williams initiative to organize an ancillary circus event at the shopping center. A Loveman's ad described the Normandale appearance as a "preview" event—six weeks to the day after the shopping center's grand opening.

Soon after the Hank Williams event, Normandale built its own portable stage for band performances, drawings for contests, and other promotional functions. One of the first to use it was Jack Turner, a locally popular singer/songwriter/ recording artist. In the early 1950s, he was a regular performer on "Deep South Jamboree," a live-in-the-studio radio show on the WBAM station

PR

*Above: Jack Turner concert in Normandale's front parking area, and as viewed from the rear—PR.*

("the Big Bam"). Among Turner's peers in central Alabama were Rebe Gosdin and Shorty Sullivan.

One of Turner's singles, "Model T Baby," was released on the RCA Victor label in early 1955, which meant that Turner's Normandale performances in that time frame were even more mutually beneficial.

In June of the same year, Turner got his own television show in Montgomery. His daughter Dixie, who sang with her father's band, was locally known for a memorable tag line for a TV show sponsor: "Mama! It's the Farm Bureau man!"

Turner's "day job" was as an artist and illustrator for Maxwell Air Force Base. A portrait he painted of Hank Williams was displayed by Hank's mother, Lillie Stone, in Hank's room in her Montgomery boarding house and would later be acquired by the Hank Williams Museum.

Following Hank Williams's death, it was rumored that Turner was being considered to portray Williams in an upcoming biopic. There was a decent resemblance between the two musicians, but nothing materialized and actor George Hamilton played Hank in the 1964 movie, *Your Cheatin' Heart.*

In addition to Country & Western bands like Jack Turner and His Singing River Boys, dance combos such as the Doug Sheehan Orchestra gave free outdoor concerts in Normandale's parking lot. Sheehan's band was a favorite among Montgomery society organizations and also performed at local venues such as the Flamingo Club on West Fairview Avenue.

THE FRANCIS CAFETERIA, LOCATED under the Doctors' Building, opened in early November 1954, and the response was enthusiastic. Eventually, civic clubs and organizations such as Toastmasters International and the Business and Professional Women's Club would utilize special private sections of the cafeteria for their meetings. Many referred to the restaurant as simply "the Francis."

Like many Montgomery youngsters, Julia Hightower (Gregg) was a big fan of "the Francis."

"Although we usually ate at home, the Francis Cafeteria was a memorable exception," she recounted, "because my grandmother, whom I loved, took me there—usually on a shopping day—and I always ordered the custard and usually

*Left: Turner's portrait of Hank Williams; Right: MGM Records publicity photo of Turner.*

the fish. Don't ask me 'why' on the fish, but the custard speaks for itself. Everything about the journey down that magical line of food choices reminds me of love and special attention."

Barry Chrietzberg, son of Parker-Sledge Hardware manager Leo Chrietzberg, recalled that stringent local "blue laws" figured into the operating hours of the restaurant. But when those were vacated, lunches at the Francis became extremely popular with members of nearby churches following Sunday morning services.

"I loved the egg custard pie at the Francis," Chrietzberg said. "In addition, I loved their shrimp cocktail. It was more expensive than most items so the server would look at my dad to see if it was all right to serve me, since I was a young boy."

In the traditional days before men's hair was cut by so-called "stylists," the Normandale Barber Shop, under the aegis of Ed Harrelson, quickly garnered regular customers. For women, Louise's Beauty Salon was next door.

For the first Holiday retail season in 1954, workers at Normandale stores received an extra Christmas present in the form of tickets to the Blue-Gray collegiate all-star football game played annually on Christmas Day in Cramton Bowl. Thanks to the sponsoring Montgomery Lions Club member Dave Larson, the Normandale Merchants' Association acquired a block of 550 tickets to the

*Above: Francis Cafeteria at Normandale—PR, and Francis's serving line image that originally appeared on a postcard— ADAH. Below: Normandale Barber Shop—ADAH.*

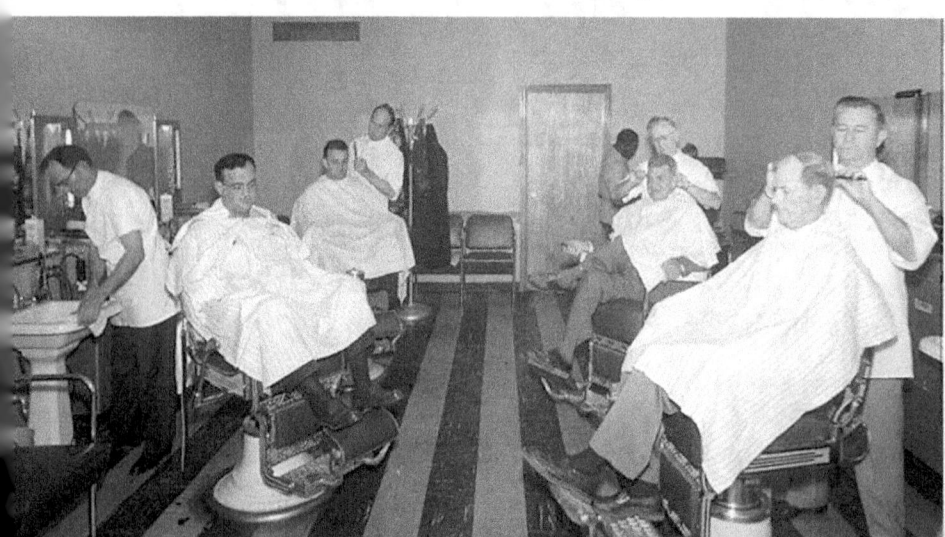

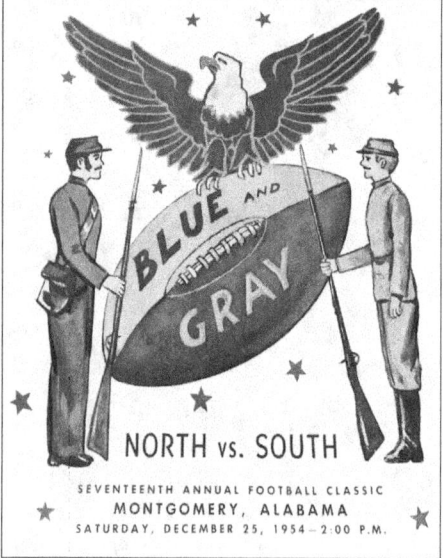

seventeenth annual event. Each employee received two tickets.

THE PLANS FOR THE new shopping center had been monitored by members of First Baptist Church downtown, who implemented a "mission" initiative that would build a new church in the large field at the corner of Patton Avenue and Norman Bridge Road across from Normandale. The new church began its worship services in the auditorium of Charles Floyd School, located a few blocks further north. The first service was held September 5, 1954—the same week that Normandale Shopping Center opened. Normandale Baptist Church received its charter as an independent church on December 5. By the fall of 1955, the new congregation had moved into vacant store spaces on the east side of Cloverland Shopping Center at 3650–3658 South Perry Street.

"My family and other families were charged with leaving First Baptist and starting Normandale Baptist," recalled Leah Larson Meacham, daughter of Dave Larson. "I can recall meeting at Cloverland until the building across from Normandale was built."

The first unit of six planned phases of construction for Normandale Baptist Church in its permanent location was a worship-educational building, which would be dedicated on November 4, 1956.

The Southern Baptist Convention wasn't the only denomination that was endeavoring to establish a foothold in proximity to Normandale Shopping Center.

Normandale Methodist Church was chartered on July 31, 1955. The congregation had begun meeting the previous month at the nearby Harrison Elementary School. Construction of a new church building later commenced on a large lot located on East Patton Avenue at Wesley Drive, which ran behind Normandale, adjacent to the shopping center's rear parking lots.

Parker-Sledge Hardware's Leo Chrietzberg was an active member of the congregation, and was elected to the church's first board of stewards.

The growth strategy of the Methodist church was similar to the Baptists'. The consecration and formal opening services for the first unit of Normandale Methodist Church took place on January 13, 1957.

~

*David Robertson probably spoke for almost any professional photographer who ever had a wedding assignment at Normandale Methodist Church, as he recalled the visual challenges in that building's sanctuary.*

*"The large stained glass window on the west side of the church created somewhat of a problem when photographing afternoon weddings," Robertson recounted. "On a sunny day, light passing through the mostly blue-and-red glass would render the bride's gown an unusual shade of magenta, not to mention the Smurf-like skin tones of the entire wedding party."*

IN DECEMBER 1954, AARON Aronov announced that Ed Dombrowski had resigned as the general manager of Normandale Shopping Center, effective at the end of the month. He was succeeded in early 1955 by another go-getter, Bill Denson, who was also a combat veteran of World War II and had been wounded at

*Bill Denson—PR.*

*Loveman's employees line up as participants in the "Casual Shopper's Days" promotion. The men's hosiery made a notable, er, fashion statement regarding the times—PR.*

the Battle of the Bulge. Denson's official title was "Executive Secretary" of the Normandale Merchants' Association.

Dombrowski's early and highly successful promotions within a six-week time frame had set the bar high, but Denson quickly demonstrated that he was up to the task. He aggressively promoted Normandale in the media. The numerous detailed and enthusiastic "news stories" Denson submitted to local media (usually with no byline) were obviously public relations articles, but they worked. He also instituted numerous on-site innovations such as "Casual Shopper's Days" (Wednesdays) and frequent giveaways, which always drew a crowd.

Drawings for merchandise usually utilized rotating eight-sided cylindrical barrels made from plywood and screen mesh. On one memorable occasion, a huge cement truck was used as a gimmick to "mix" the entries as an allusion to Normandale's progress with new construction.

One innovative drawing that was staged numerous times was the "Anything You Want" giveaway. The person whose name was drawn received his or her choice of any single item for sale within the

entire shopping center.

Some of the bigger giveaways included automobiles, in collaborations with local dealerships. Naturally, the more valuable the prizes, the more people showed up for the drawing.

The earliest drawings were usually conducted in front of the somewhat-narrow juncture between Loveman's and Mel's Photo Shop, the store at the east end of the western wing. Denson would often

*Above: Rotating contest barrel for drawings. Left: One drawing for prizes featured a cement truck whose revolving hopper mixed the entries.*

select a child (who would be blindfolded) to pull out the winning entry.

Diane Walker, the oldest of five sisters, recalled, "We lived right behind Normandale. There were so many specialty stores, and it seemed like the only stores my family could afford were Kwik Chek, Liger's, and Loveman's. But we loved window shopping at those dress shops and shoe stores.

"I would ride my bike over there with my cocker spaniel 'Floppy Jane' in my basket. I would buy an ice cream cone, and Floppy Jane always got her own ice cream cone. And, one time they were giving away gifts. Floppy Jane and I were in the crowd as they spun the basket and pulled out names. My grandmother, Pearl Bates, had filled out a lot of forms, and they called her name several times, but you only got the first gift from the first time they pulled your name. The emcee said, 'It makes you wonder whose name will be drawn for the grand prize,' and it was televised. I held my sweet Floppy Jane above my head and my family saw her on TV."

A NEW ADDITION TO the Normandale store lineup during its first year was Virginia Dare, a regional chain store that featured popular-priced clothing for women and children.

*Below: Normandale Merchants' Association participants in the award presentation to lucky winner Miss Ernestine Pearson (seated) were, left to right, Charles Wainwright Jr., Adolph Eagle, and Mel Price. She chose a sectional sofa from Loveman's as her prize. All photos this page—PR.*

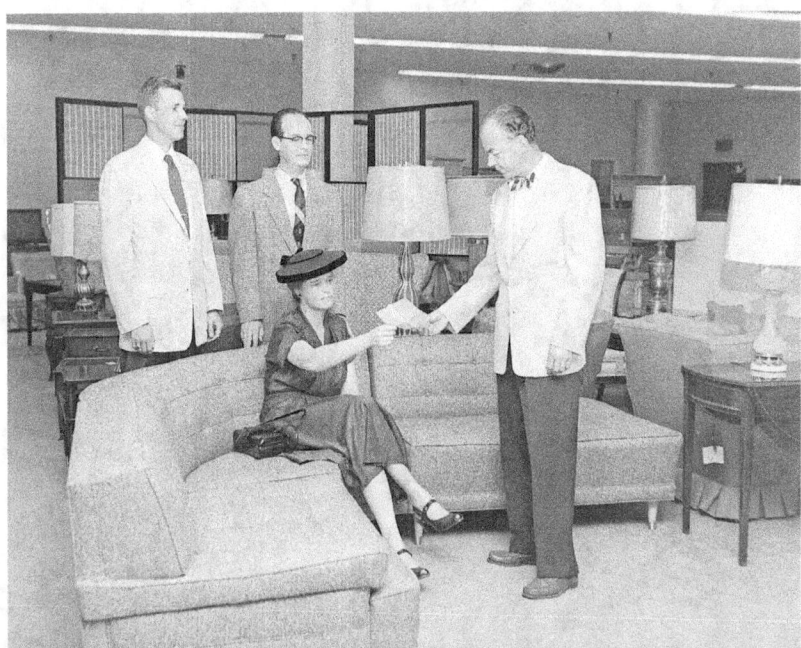

*Above: New Chevrolet giveaway, 1956; Below: Bill Denson supervises a drawing with a blindfolded youngster as an assistant; both—PR.*

That retailer moved into a space between F. W. Woolworth and Toyland in March 1955.

ON APRIL 5, 1955, voluptuous actress Cleo Moore put in a brief appearance at Normandale. Originally from Galvez, Louisiana, she was one of Hollywood's fabled 1950s "blond bombshells," most of whom were emulating standard bearer Marilyn Monroe. Moore came to Montgomery to promote a new movie, *Women's Prison,* which also starred Ida Lupino and Howard Duff. The film was playing at Montgomery's Empire Theatre, and Moore autographed photos in its lobby.

A sizeable crowd awaited Miss Moore at the shopping center. She dutifully posed for pictures and signed autographs, but it turned out that she was a camera buff, so during her visit, she spent some extra time discussing photography and color movies with a delighted Mel Price at Mel's Photo Shop. A photo of Moore that was taken during her visit to Mel's appeared in a press release and would

*Above left: Mel Price with fellow photography enthusiast Cleo Moore. Above right: On the set of WSFA-TV; both—PR. Below: Moore poses for a glamour shot in the Normandale parking lot.*

be proudly displayed in the store for years.

She also paid a visit to WSFA-TV for an in-studio live interview on a local show, "The Guest Room," hosted by Cathryn Wright. An early participant in live local television, Wright was the mother of Toni Tennille, who played piano on her mother's show and other WSFA broadcasts. Toni later achieved international success in the platinum-selling pop duo known as Captain & Tennille.

LIKE THE GRAND OPENING a year earlier, Normandale's first anniversary included a special newspaper section, "Normandale's Magnitude Still Amazes Shoppers." Several exuberant articles presented updates on retail tenants. A list of store managers included: Coleman Payne—Francis Cafeteria; Walter Darby—Darby & Sons Cleaners; Clay Crumpton—Clay Crumpton's Laundromat; Yancey Liger—Liger's Bakery; Lou Gerson—Normandale Delicatessen; Ed Harrelson—Normandale Barber Shop; Louise Finklestein—Montgomery Shoe Factory; John Thompson—City Florist; Ruth Barnes—Pauline Wilkins Candies; Harry Cohn—Loveman's; Mel Price—Mel's Photo Shop; Bernice Flack Basch—Flack's; Imogene Blackwell—DeShields-Larson Shoes; Lou Herman—Lou Herman's; Arthur Pappanastos—Capitol Clothing; C. W. Sauls—Sauls Footwear; L. B. Gordon—Toyland; Pauline Russell—Virginia Dare; R. J. Couch—F. W. Woolworth; Samuel Blankenbaker—Kwik Chek; Leo Chrietzberg—Parker-Sledge Hardware; Ford Munn Jr.—Roslyn Eagle; and C. Trimble—Lee's Drugs.

The Doctors' Building wasn't completely

occupied when Normandale opened a year earlier, but the physicians now listed as tenants: E. Fred Campbell—Internal Medicine; Jesse Ellington—Dentistry; William Farrar—Dentistry; J. H. Farrior—Eye, Ear, Nose and Throat; Conrad Walters—Obstetrics and Gynecology; Ed Webb—Pediatrics; John White—Surgery; and Kathleen Wickman—Obstetrics and Gynecology. Plans were also announced for a laboratory to be used by all tenants in the Doctors' Building.

IN THE SPRING OF 1955, the breezeway between Loveman's and Mel's Photo Shop was modified to lead to a new children's play area called "Kiddie-Land," which was created as a place for youngsters to frolic while their parents shopped. A scalloped sign was placed above the entrance.

A June 24, 1955, news release announced Kiddie-Land's opening and boosted the play area's sand boxes, wading pools, swings, slides and see-saws. Not all of the diversions were in place in late June, but a self-propelled mini choo-choo track and a "Tubs of Fun" ride were up and running.

For the first few days following Kiddie-Land's debut, a Shetland pony ride was a special addition. Free soft drinks and snow-cones were also distributed.

Kiddie-Land was also highly promoted on

*Left: Entrance to Kiddie-Land, 1955—PR. Press release photos of Kiddie-Land included a snow cone stand, a mini choo-choo, and a Tubs-of-Fun ride—note the roofline of KwIk Chek in the upper right background.*

*A crowd gathers for a nighttime drawing. Bill Denson can be seen in a light coat under the scalloped sign at the entrance to the narrow breezeway between Loveman's and Mel's Photo Shop—PR.*

Normandale's first anniversary in September 1955 (free snow cones and soft drinks again), but the play area didn't last long. The scalloped sign at its erstwhile entrance was changed to read "Choice Parking in the Rear."

PAULINE WILKINS CANDIES WAS a unique effort within a store area of approximately one thousand square feet next to the north-facing side of Loveman's. The owner had made and marketed her sweet treats out of her own kitchen in Meridian, Mississippi, starting

*Pauline Wilkins—PR.*

in 1925. Her subsequent candy-making initiatives had been in Washington, D.C., and Auburn, Alabama. She had maintained a tea room in Montgomery for seven years before opening her small shop in Normandale, where she sold sixty-five types of candy, including bon bons, marzipan, pecan brittle, and pralines. The Normandale shop also had a tea room that could seat fifty persons.

A 456-POUND BIRTHDAY CAKE in the shape of the shopping center was displayed in a Loveman's

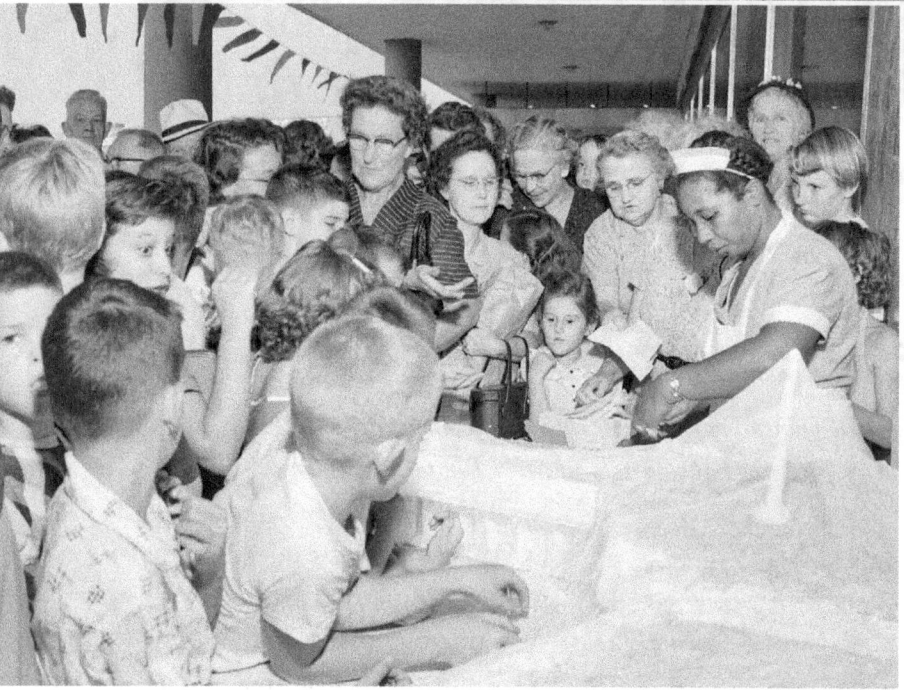

*Normandale Merchants' Association officers (top) pose with the first anniversary cake. From left: Bill Denson, Mel Price, Bernice Basch, Dave Larson, and Leo Chrietzberg. The cake was later served to customers (mostly kids)—PR.*

window. John Wilson, the head baker at Liger's, supervised the project and stated that the cake could feed 2,500 people.

In a brief interview, Normandale Merchants' Association president Dave Larson said sales for most retailers during the first year had been 20 to 40 percent higher than projected. He also cited the rapid growth in home construction in south Montgomery as part of the Normandale phenomenon.

Noting an effort to reach beyond Montgomery, a brief article in the special section estimated that half a million people lived within a two-hour drive to Normandale.

Cathryn Wright hosted a special broadcast on location for the first birthday of the shopping center. The show was proclaimed to be the first hour-long remote telecast in Montgomery. Wright's guests included musicians Jack Turner and Shorty Sullivan (who performed on separate nights at Normandale during the anniversary promotion), and a family of Seminole Indians.

During the anniversary celebration, Mel Price demonstrated a unique Polaroid Land camera at his photography supply store. "Instant" Polaroid cameras had come onto the marketplace a few years earlier, but the device at Mel's Photo Shop developed an 8 x 10-inch photo in just sixty seconds. Its retail price was $8500.

The Normandale Delicatessen offered a free cup of coffee to customers during the first anniversary celebration, but that business would become Joy's Restaurant and Fountain not long after the birthday event. The new eatery switched to a more contemporary menu.

By the first anniversary of Normandale, more than one electric kiddie ride had been placed at strategic locations along the walkway. The original company

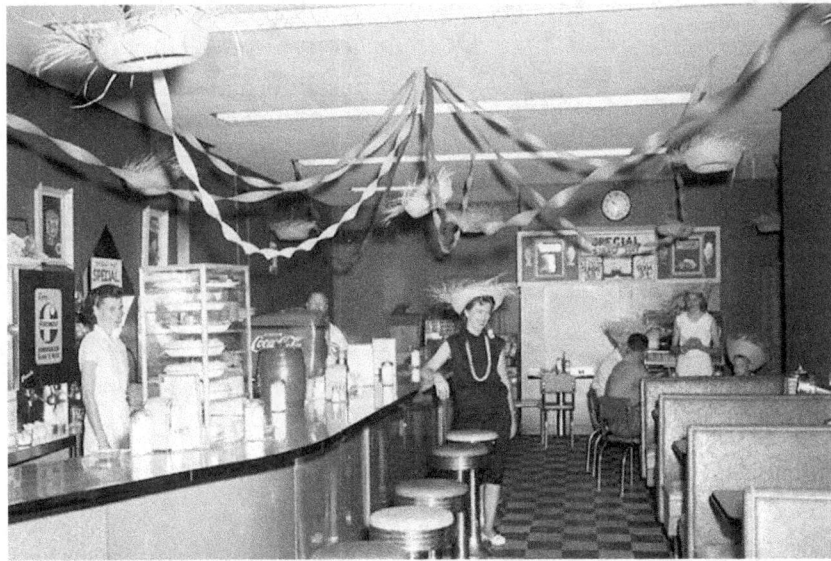

*Below: A Paul Robertson photo deduced to be from Normandale's first anniversary in 1955, with patriotic bunting on the façade. The short-lived Normandale Delicatessen, seen at the left, was apparently still open. Left: Joy's Restaurant and Fountain sported tropical straw hats during a special promotion—ADAH.*

*Placement of this Bally "Model T" kiddie ride in front of the Toyland store was a no-brainer (and 'no-brainer' didn't exist as a term back then)—PR.*

that maintained such machines wasn't Franco Distributing, but Rubin Franco and his associates later contracted with Normandale management and operated the simple nickel-per-ride diversions at the shopping center for a number of years.

ANOTHER INNOVATIVE PROMOTION WAS announced at the beginning of the Easter shopping season in

*Officials place actual diamonds in envelopes; from left, Loveman's manager Harry Cohn, Bill Denson, Police Chief Goodwyn Ruppenthal, and Police Captain Miller.—PR.*

March 1956. The "Big Diamond Hunt" contest relied on the assistance of the Montgomery Police Department and gave away real diamonds and rhinestones that were placed in individually numbered envelopes. From Thursday, March 8, through Saturday, March 10, any purchase at any Normandale store included one of the numbered envelopes containing either a gem or a gimcrack. A list of the winning numbers was announced at the close of business on Saturday.

IT WAS SOON OBVIOUS that, as Dave Larson had proclaimed, Normandale was succeeding far beyond initial projections.

"Developers came from all over the country—even from California—to see what was going on in Montgomery, Alabama," Owen Aronov said proudly. "Some people have said that Normandale was the first *regional* shopping center in the South—not 'neighborhood shopping center,' not 'community shopping center,' but '*regional*,' which meant it had a department store, grocery store, and a mix of tenants that would have a regional draw. It didn't just draw its customers from Montgomery. Even people from other states were coming to Normandale to shop on weekends."

Accordingly, plans were made for seventeen new stores that would be constructed behind Loveman's, with the same covered walkways but with differences in layout and store size.

The new section would be accessed by customers via a wider passageway beside Loveman's. The original space for Mel's Photo Shop was demolished, and the photo supply store moved west to a space on the front line that had been occupied by Wright Interiors, which had moved to a larger frontline store between City Florist and Pauline Wilkins Candies, on the other side of the new breezeway.

*Initial construction for W. T. Grant in Normandale's expansion. The deep excavation on the southern end (opposite the camera location) was the beginning of a community center/fallout shelter beneath Grant's. That's Norman Bridge Road in the background.—PR.*

Flack's, the shop next to the original Mel's, became the retailer next to the enlarged passageway.

Once again, Sherlock, Smith & Adams and Jehle Brothers Construction expeditiously handled the architecture and construction, and the second phase took shape in short order.

NORMANDALE PROMOTED ITS SECOND birthday in late August 1956 with a birthday cake claimed to weigh more than *thirteen hundred* pounds. Moreover, Liger's John Wilson had baked numerous two-dollar bills inside the cake. It was also exhibited in a Loveman's display window.

Giant festive balloons were displayed, and the Doug Sheehan Orchestra played on two nights. One announcement noted that the annual payroll for the shopping center had already surpassed one million dollars.

Yet for all of the second anniversary hoopla on the front line of Normandale, thousands of customers were speculating about what was happening in back, where the extension was being built and more free parking spots were being laid out.

Bill Denson released an informative article about the new addition, noting that most of the new stores would have more square footage than the "shops" in the front original section.

The nomenclature used by shopping center officials, retailers, and customers to describe the expansion varied. Some called the new, enlarged passageway a "breezeway," while others used the term "mall" to describe the connector section. And depending on who you asked, the new shopping area was an "arcade," a "courtyard," or a "mall." Ultimately, "arcade" seemed to win out, and retailers who opened in the new section often used the phrase "Normandale Arcade" in their advertising.

The largest store in the new section would be a W. T. Grant "junior department store," with twenty-five thousand square feet of retail space located at the opposite end of the arcade from the breezeway.

Additional clothing retailers who had reportedly signed up included a Diana's Shop, Bronson's, Chandler's Shoes, and Thom McAn. Other stores were unnamed in Bill Denson's press release/update, but the new tenants were slated to include a jewelry store, a maternity shop, an automobile parts store, a bookstore and lending library, a card and gift shop, a millinery shop and a tailoring/alterations shop. For whatever reasons, some of those commitments didn't come to fruition.

*Second anniversary giveaway prizes were displayed in a Loveman's ground-level display window. The main prize was a color television (color broadcasts were still a new phenomenon in 1956).—PR.*

Denson also used the "progress report" to cite the new People's Bank & Trust Company which was being built on the far west end of the front strip next to Lee's Drugs. The financial institution, introduced as Montgomery's fourth bank, was founded locally. Directors on its organizing board were notable Capital City businessmen: Les Weinstein, Charles Denio, Hunter Flack, Tine Davis, Ed Lowder, Oscar Covington, John Godbold, and Dave Mussafer.

The Normandale branch would feature two drive-up windows so customers could conduct bank business from their automobiles. The bank's grand opening ceremony was held Thursday, January 24, 1957.

# 5

# Santa Claus Is Coming to Mount Olympus

Jolly Old St. Nick began collaborating with Normandale regarding his annual obligations during the shopping center's first Christmas shopping season in 1954, and some unique facets to his initial appearance would carry over to future arrivals too.

In the early days of Normandale, Santa's arrival date and time were announced in advance. The event would usually draw a huge crowd of youngsters and parents to the front of Loveman's.

However, Santa wasn't transported to Normandale via his traditional reindeer-powered sleigh (and snow was never a factor). Normandale had Santa chauffeured to his duty station by the Montgomery Fire Department. A large fire engine's loud, roaring motor and blaring siren revved up the kids' excitement even more. Once he arrived, St. Nick was escorted to other stores by firemen before reporting for duty at Loveman's.

Santa's highly visible station in the right-facing second-floor display window of Loveman's was an unforgettable sight for children and shoppers for many years. The icon surveyed Normandale's front parking lot like some modern-day, omnipotent Yuletide Zeus gazing down from Mt. Olympus (albeit from behind a giant plate glass window).

*Christmas shopping season, 1954: This image shows a clear view of the original smaller passageway to the rear of the shopping center, where Kiddie-Land would be set up in mid-1955— ADAH.*

*Santa arrives via fire truck and is greeted by large crowds of enthusiastic youngsters—PR.*

*Above, left, firemen escorting Santa; right, night view of Santa in his usual station on Loveman's second floor.—ADAH. Bottom, early sleigh-on-tracks display; inset, 1956 tree installation—both, PR.*

Santa would patiently listen to children's requests as they sat on his lap and told him of their desires for Christmas toys. Parents would usually have their offspring photographed with Santa as well. As Christmas approached, the shopping center's stores would stay open every night until 9 p.m. The changed hours were noted in Normandale's holiday advertising.

One early outdoor Christmas display was a cute train on a short track, installed on the northwest corner of the shopping center's adjacent to the intersection of Norman Bridge Road and Patton Avenue.

THE 1956 CHRISTMAS SEASON would be particularly memorable, as the lighted tree installed at Normandale was proclaimed to be the tallest in the world.

The press releases hyping the gigantic Norwegian spruce recounted that it was purchased from a tree farm in New Jersey and shipped to Montgomery on three railroad cars. It measured 101½ feet from the tip of the decorative star to its base, and the circumference of the trunk was ten feet, six inches. It weighed more than 17,000 pounds and was 13 feet taller than that year's Christmas tree at Rockefeller Center in New York City. The electrical wiring for its hundreds of lights stretched approximately 12,600 feet—that's more than two miles of electrical cord.

*Above: A crowd gathers for the 6 p.m. November 30, 1956, tree lighting. The still-under-construction People's Bank & Trust building is in the background, adjacent to Lee's Cut-Rate Drugs. Below: Santa blesses the attendees. The videographer next to him is Laurens Pierce. Both photos—PR.*

Santa also showed up for the proceedings and gave treats and souvenirs to youngsters. A Girl Scout troop sang Christmas carols. Laurens Pierce was on hand to film the proceedings, while Paul Robertson took photographs. Pierce used a modified Bolex 16mm movie camera. "Laurens was known for his inventive nature, especially when it came to his movie camera," David Robertson recalled. "Since the tree lighting event was after dark, Laurens added what appears to be a homemade attachment for lighting."

*Above, youngsters at the tree-lighting got treats from Santa. Below, throwing the tree-lighting switches were Mayor W. A. Gayle and his*

EARLY IN NORMANDALE'S HISTORY, Loveman's began a Christmas tradition of constructing expansive animated "Magic of Christmas" scenes in its ground floor display windows, showcasing mechanical figures that were in motion (not unlike the "It's a Small World" attraction that would be introduced by the Walt Disney company in the mid-1960s). Loveman's

*granddaughter Kathy, Maxwell Air Force Base wing commander Colonel Mills Savage, Loveman's store manager Harry Cohn, and Bill Denson. Bottom, the lit tree! All photos—PR.*

wasn't the only retail chain to offer such a tableau, but its display was a favorite at Normandale during the Christmas season.

The memory of "the Normandale Santa Claus" seated on his throne upstairs at Loveman's was unforgettable for thousands of children.

"In conversations with people about my age, the prevailing topic that leaps forward concerning Normandale is Santa," said David Robertson. "The shopping center definitely knew how to capitalize on the excitement and joy associated with this seasonal character. The Toyland store was a storehouse for every possible item Santa would need to please a young child, but there was an abundance of other consumer delights awaiting shoppers in this unique combination of stores."

# 6

# Expansion and Competition

The Normandale expansion was completed in early 1957. The new breezeway was eye-catching, with pennants fluttering on three tall flagpoles at the entrance and curved, translucent panels furnishing a type of rolling/corduroy skylight effect. In later years, the silhouette of the three-pennant look would appear in more than one of the shopping center's logos.

Pay telephones in the smaller passageway when Kiddie-Land was viable were replaced by small glass display cases on the side walls when the enlarged breezeway was completed. Bicycle racks were placed at strategic locations throughout the shopping center. One rack was in the middle of the new breezeway, displaying a sign admonishing youngsters to park their bikes

*Entrance to Normandale's new arcade (ADAH) and the new Toyland location it contained (PR).*

there. However, store owners and their employees still had to chastise kids who rode their bikes on the walkway. "My memories include riding bikes on the sidewalks and having merchants yell at me," one former youngster said of his Normandale experiences.

With the new addition constructed, Toyland and Roslyn Eagle relocated from the front line to the arcade.

The arcade's planned automotive parts store, which turned out to be a Western Auto, ended up

*Above: Interior shots from the new breezeway, looking in towards the arcade and outwards towards the original front line of stores. Note the small glass display cases mounted on the walls and the parking rack for bicycles—ADAH. Below, left, northwest view of the center of the arcade, and right, southwest view of the center of the arcade—PR.*

on the western front line, next to Lee's Drugs in the space vacated by Roslyn Eagle when that furniture store moved to the arcade.

The main shopping area of the new arcade was rectangular, with clothing and shoe stores taking up a majority of the layout. Other stores were Norman Jewelers, Toyland, Roslyn Eagle, W. T. Grant, and F. W. Woolworth, still with the red letters of its signage. The new Woolworth's was not open when the expansion debuted in early March 1957; it remained next to Kwik Chek on the front line until the arcade store's grand opening was announced in early August.

MANY OF THE NEW stores had been mentioned by name in the "progress report" released during the second anniversary celebration and/or during the 1956 year-end update article.

Bronson's hyped its "Store of Individual Shops" concept, in which sections catered to specific customers. Examples included the "Varsity Shop" (young men and boys) and the "Career Shop" (junior-size women's apparel).

The center open area of the arcade had several large brick planters—circular flower beds that were eighteen inches tall, allowing for merchandise exhibits and/or displays of decorative plants. A circular fountain graced the entrance to the open area.

The thirteen-foot high canopy over the walkways in the arcade was three feet higher than the canopy in the original front line, but was still fifteen feet wide. The small signs suspended from the ceiling of the walkways were illuminated but still simple.

*Esther Fleischman (right) proffers a ring to a customer at Norman Jewelers; a sign to the right of the displayed 1958 Chevy wagon pointed would-be customers toward several smaller shops off the main arcade—PR.*

Norman Jewelers was located on the northeast corner of the open air portion of the annex. The Record Shop, the Maternity Shop, Mark Hall (cards and gifts), Bill's Beauty Shop, and Yutmeyer Photography were smaller retailers in an ancillary passageway off the southwest side of Loveman's. Despite what some retailers anticipated would be less pedestrian traffic in that offshoot section, Loveman's still maintained mannequins in window displays located on that side. Ultimately, a sign was posted listing the retailers in that section, with an arrow pointing in the direction of the shops, which were smaller than the stores in the arcade's main section. The beauty parlor changed owners in early 1960 and became known as the Style-Art Beauty Salon.

THE COMBINATION COMMUNITY CENTER and fallout shelter that had been built underneath the W. T. Grant store at the rear of the arcade could reportedly accommodate several hundred persons. Normandale management advised the public that the community center would be available for club meetings and other events. A local Boy Scout troop took advantage, as did an organization of amateur thespians known as the Montgomery Little Theater, which quickly began staging plays in the facility.

Longtime Montgomery dance instructor Billy Pinkston taught classes in the facility beneath Grant's. "I took dance lessons with Billy Pinkston in the basement studio," recalled Julia Hightower Gregg. "Afterwards, I'd go upstairs and buy fruit gummies from the candy counter. I can still remember the sunsets when I came up from those after-school sessions—acrobatics, ballet, and tap. I *do* remember that at age thirteen I broke my two front teeth in a fall—a foiled tour jeté move. So graceful . . ."

Pinkston's reputation extended to the then unincorporated Pike Road area.

"In my junior high school days, 1959 to 1962, he taught a group of us kids at Pike Road School how to do the cha-cha," recalled George Howell. "For country teenagers, this was really different! For a month or so, Pinkston came to Pike Road about once a week, put on his records, and we learned a cha-cha routine. I paired up one afternoon with a girl I really liked, and I was very surprised at how stiffly she danced. It turned out that Pinkston was putting on an outdoor recital with his Montgomery dance students. So, one springtime Friday night, the group from Pike Road got to put on their best clothes, go to Normandale, and dance the cha-cha on the asphalt parking lot under the stars, somewhere out in front of Kwik Chek. I never knew who arranged the lessons, who paid for them, or why, but it was fun to be at Normandale at night!"

Pinkston's Normandale location may have been advantageous, but

*Dave Larson, below, and right with performers from the Vicki Atkins Dancing School in Tallassee. Left to right, front: Lisa Griffith, Charlene Hill, Patti Moncrief; Back: Joy Harris, Phyllis Nix, Brenda Johnson, LeAnne Estes.— courtesy of Vicki Baker*

most of the attention to dance in Montgomery was provided by Dave Larson of DeShields-Larson Shoes. By the late 1950s, local youngsters were referring to the co-owner of the store as "Uncle Dave" Larson. His merchandise had diversified into dancing shoes, leotards, tights, ballerina outfits, and dance hosiery. He began hosting a weekly program on WCOV-TV called *Dancing Dolls*, which endeared him to youngsters and parents even more.

Of course, DeShields-Larson Shoes sponsored the TV show, and the retailer let it be known that students taught by specific instructors or schools would be seen on the show. A 1957 listing of such dance schools and teachers included Molly Brumby, Normandale Dance Studio, Loree Atkins Davis, Betty Pyron, Jackie Rocheleaur, and Helen Thorington.

Dance schools endorsed by the show varied from year to year. By the early 1960s, some of the original schools were no longer listed but performers were noted as students from other schools,

See Uncle Dave's *Dancing Dolls* Featured On **WCOV-TV** 5:30–6:00 P.M. **Every Thursday**

SEE FIRST SHOW THURSDAY, AUG. 30

UNCLE DAVE

including Vicki Atkins Dancing School (in Tallassee), Gardner Ann Coleman Studio of the Dance, McConnell Twins Dance Studio, Lucie Stone's School of Ballet, Willadean Walden School of Dance, Mr. Lynn Curtis Dancing School, Mann Dance Studio, and Mrs. Ned Woodall Studio of the Dance (in Tallassee and Wetumpka).

Vicki Atkins's older sister Loree had also taught dance for Billy Pinkston in Normandale's community center before opening her own studio in Montgomery. Another sister, Julia, opened a dance school in Prattville.

And Vicki herself was operating her own Tallassee school when she was fifteen years old. "Our tap shoes, our dance shoes and our ballet shoes all came from DeShields-Larson in Normandale," she recalled. "Mr. Larson was always very personable, and the kids just loved him because he always encouraged them. A lot of the girls were nervous when they got there but he had a positive effect on them. It was always exciting for the kids, and some still talk about it today. We were on that show for several years."

"Daddy often used (sister) Lisa or me as models," said Leah Larson Meacham, "but I don't think either of us ever danced on the show!"

IN THE MID-1950S, MONTGOMERY'S retail activity was moving northeasternly, and by mid-1956, two smaller shopping centers were under construction in the Atlanta Highway/State Coliseum area.

Eastbrook was developed on Coliseum Boulevard by the Eastbrook Land Company. The architects were Pearson, Tittle, and Narrows, and the shopping center was built by Bear Brothers Construction Company, with Smith and Cochran Realty as rental agents. Construction began in mid-summer 1956 and was completed in early 1957, paralleling the timeline of the expansion at Normandale.

The new eastside facility had a straight-line thirteen-store assemblage, The assignment of a Montgomery Fair store as the anchor unit in the center of the lineup was a huge plus. A W. T. Grant store was on one end of the line and a Piggly Wiggly grocery

*Below, Eastbrook construction, late 1956. Bottom, the completed retail center. Both—ADAH.*

*Newlyweds head out for a honeymoon following their reception in the Gold Room of the Montgomery Fair in Eastbrook—PR.*

was on the other end. Other retailers included siblings of Normandale tenants—F. W. Woolworth, Parker-Sledge Hardware, and Sauls Footwear.

Also in the original incarnation of Eastbrook were the Carousel Gift and Record Shop, Renfroe's, Four Seasons, Lerner Shop, Toytown, Jay's Shoe Store, Rosemont Gardens Flower Shop, Rexall Drugs, Freehling's Store for Children, and Country Kitchen restaurant.

Unlike Normandale, Eastbook faced stores across the street, on the eastern side of Coliseum Boulevard. Other stores were in development on that side, and the establishment of two gas stations and a post office on that side was noted in advance publicity.

Eastbrook's design emulated Normandale's

sheltered outdoor walkways. Moreover, the Montgomery Fair anchor store's façade had the International styling of Loveman's, but only on its left-facing side. The structure had similar straight-line-and-overhanging aesthetics, but there was only one giant display window upstairs.

Eastbrook's three-hundred-seat "Gold Room" was obviously inspired by Normandale's below-ground community center, and it also was available to the public for meetings, conferences and events. But the Eastbrook variant was part of the central Montgomery Fair structure, and it was accessible via two private entrances—one from outside and one from inside the store.

Not surprisingly, a special section on Eastbrook appeared in local newspapers on Opening Day, April 11. The subtitle of the lead story cheerily referred to the new shopping center as being located "on the morning side of town."

As IF AARON ARONOV and associates didn't have enough to monitor between the expansion work at Normandale plus the emergence of Eastbrook as a competitor, another Aronov-sponsored retail structure, Forest Hills Shopping Center, was under construction just down the road from Eastbrook.

However, the Forest Hills Shopping Center wasn't particularly a direct response to the construction of Eastbrook. Montgomery developers were already aware of the city's eastward growth, and Aronov Realty saw an opportunity to develop an eastside residential subdivision along with a smaller-scale, "neighborhood"

shopping center that was still inspired by the larger Normandale facility.

One notable accomplishment of Aronov's Forest Hills initiative was the sale of forty-nine houses in forty-eight hours. The company quickly hyped those numbers in advertisements.

Construction on Forest Hills began in late September 1956. Located at the intersection of Coliseum Boulevard and Atlanta Highway, the new center had twelve stores. The anchor unit was a Delchamps grocery, at eighteen thousand square feet the largest store the chain had built in Montgomery. It was located on the east-facing side of the shopping center. The straight-on lineup of stores had canopied walkways.

The owner of the new center was the Forest Corporation. Once again, the architects for the project were Sherlock, Smith & Adams, the general contractor was Jehle Brothers Construction, and the leasing agent was Aronov Realty Company.

*Forest Hills Shopping Center—ADAH.*

Original businesses included Cameraland (a Mel Price venture), Seawell's Shoes, Darby & Sons Cleaners, Forest Hills Barber Shop, Lee's Cut-Rate Drugs, Toyland, the Dutch Bake Shop, Tommy's Dress Shop, Casual Living gift and card shop, a beauty parlor, and another Francis Cafeteria.

Of course, the Forest Hills Shopping Center garnered a special newspaper section for its grand opening on Monday, March 19 (three weeks and two days before Eastbrook's grand opening).

~

*Cordell's Restaurant, a popular eatery that had a catchy slogan of "Eat Well With Bill Cordell," was also at the intersection of Coliseum Boulevard and the Atlanta Highway. He later moved his business to the Mobile Highway on the other side of Montgomery. Cordell's daughter Kathryn became a NASA scientist and flew on four Space Shuttle missions.*

*Miss Marian McKnight of South Carolina, 1957.*

# 7

# There She Is...

The retail environment in Montgomery was indeed expanding rapidly, and just two years after Normandale opened, Aaron Aronov's keystone retail establishment was being challenged to maintain its dominant position in central Alabama.

Accordingly, the mega-center in south Montgomery reinforced its king-of-the-mountain status in early 1957 with a promotional event that pre-empted the grand openings of the Eastbrook and Forest Hills shopping centers. Not unexpectedly, the promotion was coordinated with the debut of the new Normandale expansion. To many merchants and customers, it was the greatest and most memorable event in Normandale's history.

FOR ALL OF THE glitz, hype, proliferation and evolution of beauty pageants in the United States, the original Miss America contest on the Boardwalk in Atlantic City is still the pinnacle. Millions recall the annual television broadcast of the event hosted by singer/radio announcer/actor Bert Parks. Every year, his rendition of "There She Is, Miss America" was an iconic concluding salute to the newly crowned beauty queen.

And the reigning Miss America visited Montgomery in 1957 to lend luster to the grand opening of Normandale's new arcade. Marian McKnight of South

Carolina was crowned Miss America 1957 on September 8, 1956, and Normandale officials immediately began planning to bring her to Montgomery to cut the ribbon at the opening ceremony on March 7, 1957.

A Normandale press release/ad touted the upcoming ceremony:

AMERICA'S MOST BEAUTIFUL TO CROWN NORMANDALE QUEEN OF SHOPPING CITIES
Miss Marian McKnight, Miss America 1957, will crown Normandale as "Queen of the Shopping Cities" here Thursday. The famous South Carolina

*This Pauline Wilkins Candies ad celebrating the addition of Normandale's arcade, was published on the day of Miss America's visit.*

55

*These Dodge automobiles helped to spread the word about Miss America's visit. Note the individuals inside the new breezeway installing new glass display cases. Below left, fabled photographer/videographer Laurens Pierce and Rachel Folsom, standing to his left, are among those awaiting Miss America at Dannelly Field. Right, Marian McKnight arrives. —All, PR.*

beauty, who won 11 beauty titles before becoming Miss America, will arrive here via Delta Air Lines, Flight 315 at 2:18 Wednesday for the big Normandale opening Thursday. She will cut the ribbon opening the beautiful Normandale addition at 10 a.m. Thursday. As America's most beautiful woman, Normandale planners believed she was the only appropriate person in the country to cut the ribbon opening the new addition to America's most beautiful shopping center.

Vital Statistics on Miss America—Talents: Pianist, Dancing, Dramatics. Height: 5 ft. 5 inches, Bust: 35, Waist: 23, Weight: 120, Hips: 35, Hair: Blonde, Eyes: Blue, Age: 19

A press release focused on Normandale's retail accomplishments in the two and a half years since

*Above left, Teri Aronov, Aaron's daughter, presents McKnight with a corsage as Dave Larson looks on; above, McKnight and Rachel Folsom in their chauffeured automobile; below, with Rachel's father, Governor Jim Folsom, at the Capitol —PR.*

*Right, State Public Safety Director Bill Lyerly serving as the security escort for McKnight, who was interviewed backstage by WSFA-TV's Cathryn Wright; below, police officer directing traffic; bottom, Laurens Pierce climbed onto a ladder to get a better camera angle; — PR.*

*The temporary stage with Miss America seated on her "throne" surrounded by officials and dignitaries.*

the shopping center opened, referencing all of the employees from all stores, including estimated numbers of new employees for the new stores in the arcade. The release proclaimed that Normandale had some eight hundred regular employees and close to one thousand during the Christmas shopping season.

Paul Robertson photographed the two-day event, starting with the arrival of Miss America at Montgomery's Dannelly Field. Robertson took pictures of an enthusiastic crowd that had gathered, which included his peer and friend, Laurens Pierce, who was filming the event with his Bolex 16mm camera. Rachel Folsom, a daughter of Alabama Governor "Big Jim" Folsom, was on hand to welcome Miss McKnight, as were Aaron Aronov and his family. Aaron's daughter Teri presented a corsage to the beauty queen.

The governor had provided a chauffeured automobile for McKnight, and its first stop was at his office downtown for photos.

McKnight was then driven to the Jefferson Davis Hotel. She later visited Normandale for dinner at the Francis Cafeteria. Her security escort during her visit was Bill Lyerly, director of the State Department of Public Safety.

At the next day's ribbon-cutting ceremony, local police had an arduous dual purpose—to direct traffic and also keep the enormous crowd on the walkway and out of the parking lot to allow a limited amount of traffic flow for automobiles.

As the event began at the scheduled time of 10 a.m., McKnight was regally dressed and sitting on a temporary "throne" in Normandale's newly enlarged breezeway.

The ceremony included an invocation by the Reverend R. H. Falwell Jr. of Normandale Baptist Church, and remarks from Mayor Gayle and Dave

Larson, who was representing the Normandale Merchants' Association. Other noteworthy attendees included several military officials from Maxwell Air Force Base.

The ribbon cutting went off exactly as planned, to the delight of everyone in attendance. Montgomery's two television stations, WSFA-TV and WCOV-TV, covered the event. Numerous photographers and videographers were in attendance, and in an interesting maneuver, Laurens Pierce stationed himself at the top of a tall ladder to get a bird's-eye view.

McKnight spent the rest of the day visiting Normandale stores and ate her second meal at the Francis Cafeteria. Following a clothing change back at her hotel in late afternoon, she returned to Normandale for dinner, and completed her visits to retailers, as a throng of well-wishers followed her from store to store. It was a long but memorable day for McKnight and her fans in central Alabama.

Miss America's visit to Montgomery was a rousing success, and many store owners and patrons of Normandale would never forget the occasion. It was considered a high point of the retail history of the Capital City.

As NOTED EARLIER, SEVERAL automobiles furnished by the local dealership, John Boswell Dodge, were decorated with crepe paper ribbon and publicity posters. The vehicles were then dispatched to cruise throughout the greater Montgomery area to promote the upcoming event.

Another Dodge, a Coronet model, was on display in the new breezeway. To many classic automobile aficionados, the 1957 Dodge Coronet would be considered a definitive example of the late fifties' kitschy automobile styles—two-tone paint job, white sidewall tires, different-size headlights, lots of chrome, and, of course, space-era tailfins.

The display Coronet was given away as part of the hoopla for the grand opening of Normandale's new arcade and McKnight's appearance. The drawing was held on Saturday, March 16. The snappy red-and-white vehicle was won by Rufus Stagner.

345 HP
ADVENTURER

# DE SOTO

*"The Most Exciting Car In The World Today"*

Will Be At Normandale All Week

## SOUTH'S LARGEST AUTO SHOW

This brilliant new car is so superbly styled, so perfectly powered—and manufactured with such precise quality—that only a relative few can be built. If you wish a car distinctively different from any other car on the road today, we suggest that you stop in soon to test-drive the DeSoto AD-VENTURER!

*Top, crowd at the drawing for a 1957 Dodge on March 16th. Above, the Stagner family is presented the keys to their new Dodge Coronet by Adolph Eagle; right, contest winner Rufus Stagner with his new car. —PR.*

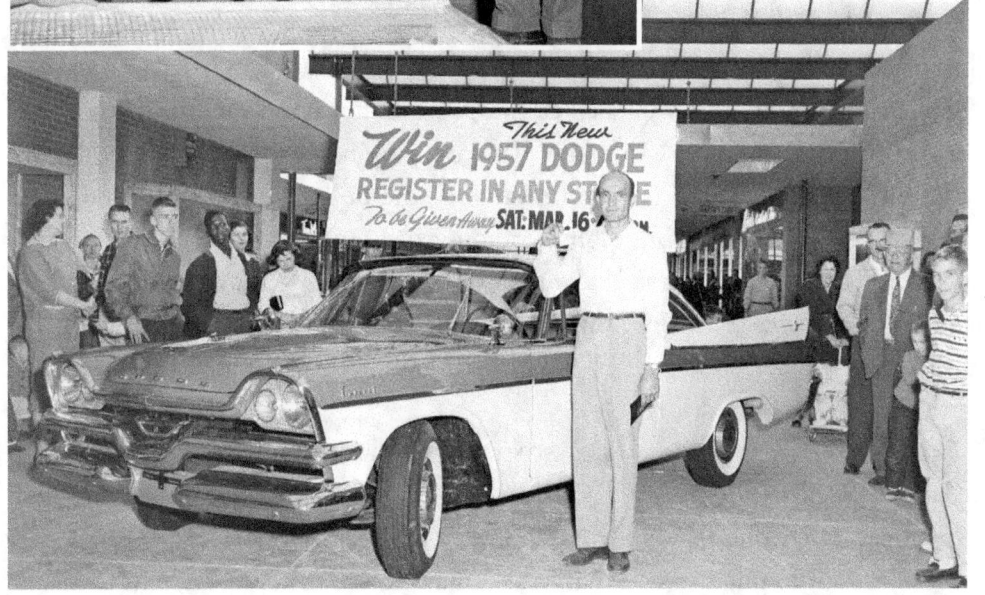

61

# (Massive) Business as Usual

The festivities regarding the addition of the arcade weren't over.

In late June, Normandale staged an automobile show. Local dealership C. E. Pitts Motors displayed used cars on the walkway near the Western Auto store. Some of the vehicles appeared to be bona fide antiques. The owner of the dealership went by the nickname of "Big-Hearted Pete," and among the new brands he sold was the French-made Renault line; the Renault Dauphine economy model would be the focus of a unique promotion two years later.

F. W. WOOLWORTH'S GRAND OPENING for its new location in the Normandale arcade was held on August 8. The new store was "double the size" of the original store, according to the press release. More square footage meant more types of merchandise, including home-oriented items such as draperies and curtains. The thirty-five-seat luncheonette was also cited, as was the store's air-conditioning.

There were five red-letter signs outside the new store, and all read "Woolworth's" instead of "F. W. Woolworth."

The original F. W. Woolworth store on the front line would be occupied by Miller's, a high-end women's clothier with a thriving fur department. "My mother was raised with five sisters," David Robertson recalled, "and her father worked on an automobile assembly line. So in her teenage years, her clothes were either hand-me-downs or hand-made. This upbringing made her very conscious of the value of the dollar, so she would not even consider going into an upscale store like Miller's. However, one Christmas Santa treated her to a mink stole. She was even brave enough to wear it in public on a few special occasions."

TO SOME OBSERVERS, THE subsequent grand openings of Eastbrook and Forest Hills—and even Normandale's third anniversary event later that year—may have seemed a bit anti-climactic compared to the March 1957 opening of the Normandale expansion—how do you top an appearance by Miss America?

Nevertheless, a special newspaper section promoting Normandale's birthday was again published. It was replete with public relations articles and special sales, as promoted by Loveman's store manager Harry Cohn, now the president of the Normandale Merchants' Association. A new innovation for the birthday promotion was a "Treasure Chest" contest, with lucky keys. Once again, a three-quarter-ton birthday cake loaded with dollar bills was baked.

A new store, Teens 'N Tweens, had opened in

*Top of facing page, the lineup of C. E. Pitts autos—ADAH. Above, Woolworth's impressive new facade, and left, Miller's display window—PR.*

early August and was promoted with a large ad and a public relations article in the anniversary special section. Another venture of Lou Herman, Teens 'N Tweens was a specialty retailer that catered exclusively to junior high and high school girls, ages eleven to seventeen. It was said to be the first store of its type in the state.

After the anniversary events, a "$20,000 Jackpot" promotion stretched across the last three months of the year. A collaboration between the Normandale Merchants' Association and Kwik Chek stores, the initiative offered tickets to customers at any Normandale store or any Kwik Chek store in Montgomery. The drawing was held on Christmas Eve at the shopping center, and participants included Mayor Gayle and Fire Chief Bob Lampley. An added attraction during the final week was the regionally popular "Trobie the Clown and His Famous Dog Act."

The grand prize was a 1958 Cadillac valued at $7,500 (about $45,000 in 2025). The winner of

the contest reportedly had been driving a 1953 Oldsmobile. Second prize was a furniture package from Loveman's for four rooms. Third prize was a mink stole from Miller's. There were thirty-four other prizes.

LATE THAT FALL, AN eighteen-foot-tall Santa was temporarily erected for the first time in the open air portion of Normandale's new arcade. The statue was equipped with a speaker system so it could "talk" with youngsters.

Decades later, one former patron opined that the placement of the talking Santa statue inside the arcade had been shrewd marketing; shoppers would need to walk into the open air section to get to the large figure and would have to pass new stores with window displays. What's more, the statue was located near Toyland and stores that sold children's clothing.

There may have been a bit of confusion among parents shopping in Normandale regarding the "Toyland" moniker the Loveman's chain used to describe its toy department. "Toyland" was also the name of an independent retailer in the shopping center. Such overlap didn't matter to the youngsters who were the primary target market of both Toylands.

BEFORE THE ARCADE OPENED, the total retail square footage on Normandale's front line was 186,000 square feet. With the expansion now open and thriving, Normandale boasted that its total retail space was 330,000 square feet.

*Facing page, a boy rides a big lion inside Toyland. Top left, the talking Santa statue installed in the Normandale arcade in 1957; top right and left, ads promote the "talking" Santa statue and validate Santa's arrival, the "Toyland" moniker for Loveman's toy department, and the store's special Christmas displays. —PR.*

*Above, Lou Herman operated three clothing stores in Normandale. Above right, Fannie Ledbetter worked at Teens 'N Tweens and at the Village Store, for a total of thirty plus years with the Herman-owned shops. Right, Village Store employees Ethel Daughtry and Hilda Calzone. —PR*

# 9

# Almost a Self-Contained City

From the outset of Normandale's history, numerous legendary merchants and stores built legacies at the retail showplace.

Lou Herman, assisted by his wife, Marjorie, marketed clothing from three different stores in Normandale—his eponymously named first store sold children's clothing, while Teens 'N Tweens, as previously noted, went after a specific demographic of girls ages 11–17, and The Village Store catered to adult women.

Like many of his shopping center peers, Herman served as the president of the Normandale Merchants' Association. All four of the Herman children—Judy, Stanley, David, and Michael—worked at the family-owned stores during their teenage years, doing stock and office work.

The Normandale community center underneath W. T. Grant later figured into Herman's clothing enterprises. "Our dad briefly had a girls' dressmaking business, Judy Lynn Originals, in one of the side rooms around the mid-1960s," said Stanley.

Suzanne Sisson (Burroughs) worked for the Herman group of stores more than once, and had meaningful memories of her experiences:

"Mr. Herman was a very good employer who taught me many things, and he stressed the importance of a good work ethic. He was stern but fair. I remember the first or second day I was there, I had to wrap a mink coat from the Village Store, and I forgot to detach the 'no-go tag' from it. The alarm went off as the customer was going out the door. Mr. Herman explained to the customer that I was new and apologized to him. I fixed the problem. I just knew I would be fired, but after I wrapped the gift again and the customer was gone, all Mr. Herman said was, 'You will not make that mistake again.' I didn't, and I continued doing everything from stuffing envelopes in the office for mail outs to tagging and steaming new clothing for the sales floor."

A few years later, Sisson again worked part-time with Herman to repay funeral expenses for Sisson's father: "After college I came back to Montgomery in 1975 and I went to work at the People's Bank and Trust Company that was on the end of the (west front line) building. I also went back to work with Mr. Herman in 1977, because my father had passed and we did not have enough money to pay for funeral expenses. I worked out a plan where I would work with Mr. Herman after my bank job at five o'clock every evening until the nine o'clock closing, and all day on Saturday, until he was paid back in full. I appreciated his kindness and the work ethic he bestowed on me at an early age."

WHILE HER STATUS AS a female in the retail ownership and management environment wasn't extensively hyped in Normandale publicity, Bernice Flack Basch was a pioneering member of that category, and sometimes her full name was used in publicity articles.

*Right, Bernice Flack Basch—P.R. Below, Madison DeShields, in Homberg hat and with a cigarette, strikes a debonair pose outside the Alex Rice store in downtown Montgomery in the early twentieth century—photo courtesy of Leah Larson Meacham. Opposite page, 1934 shoe ad.*

Originally from California, Basch moved to Montgomery in 1945 and had operated a small shop in Cloverdale before committing to the original front line of Normandale under the trade name of Flack's LTD. Basch had been oriented toward women's sportswear and ready-to-wear, but her Normandale store ultimately sold dressier, better-grade women's fashions and accessories. Basch regularly traveled to fashion shows and other events in California, New York, and Texas in search of new lines. She also pursued the wedding dress business, relying on employee Dovie Ballentine who was experienced in sales to that market segment.

Basch was a part of the Normandale Merchants' Association from its inception and served as its first treasurer.

As NOTED EARLIER, DAVE LARSON of DeShields–Larson Shoes made his mark on Normandale and its potential customers from the get-go, and his gregarious personality and ubiquitous presence at promotional events served the shopping center well for years. However, many if not most Normandale customers probably didn't know who the "DeShields" in the store name was.

For many years, Madison DeShields, Larson's father-in-law, ran the shoe department inside Alex Rice, one of the preeminent clothing retailers in downtown Montgomery. However, Alex Rice did not actually own DeShields's

enterprise. The footwear section was an independently leased retail department—a store inside a larger store. Ads would be headlined with the Alex Rice logo, with "DeShield's Shoe Dept." underneath.

In the late 1940s, Dave Larson was in the U.S. Air Force and was stationed in Montgomery. He had met DeShields's daughter Louise on a blind date. The Larsons' daughter Leah Larson Meacham said that her parents' honeymoon was a one-way trip to Chicago where Dave had taken a job in a jewelry store. "Mother hated Chicago," Meacham recounted. "My grandfather bought a car, drove it to Chicago, and told my father, 'This car is yours if you bring my daughter home, and you'll have a job, too.' So that's how DeShields–Larson Shoes got started."

The new business was structured so that Madison would remain in the leased Alex Rice section, while Dave would develop and manage the Normandale store. Larson oversaw the addition of a third store when Eastbrook Shopping Center opened in east Montgomery in late February 1958. The downtown business moved to Montgomery Street in 1960. "Daddy also opened up stores in Pensacola and Tuscaloosa," Leah recalled.

The Larsons quickly became active members of the Normandale community. "We were charter members of Normandale Baptist Church," Leah recalled, "which was across the street from the shopping center, and was built around the same time. Daddy joined the Lions Club, and became its president for three years, which meant he did a lot of work with the Blue-Gray Game. The managers of our stores were like family, and we always had a store party in the summer after we got a lake house. Daddy would also hire women to be managers, so that was ahead of its time."

LEO CHRIETZBERG, CO-OWNER OF Parker-Sledge Hardware, was an early and enthusiastic Normandale promoter.

A convivial sales veteran, Chrietzberg had worked for Teague Hardware, a large wholesaler in downtown Montgomery, for a number of years before his military service during World War II. When he returned, he worked at Parker-Sledge Hardware just off Court Square. Chrietzberg's son Barry said that his father convinced store owner George "Bubber" Bailey that Parker-Sledge needed to expand to the growing south Montgomery, so the Normandale store was created as a partnership between Bailey and Chrietzberg.

Leo spent almost a year preparing to open the new store. He helped create the Normandale Merchants' Association and was elected its first vice-president. His involvement with the establishment and construction of Normandale Methodist Church also kept him busy.

*Andy Thompson, right, was a popular early employee of Mel's Photo Shop—PR.*

MEL'S PHOTO SHOP WAS a unique business for a shopping center, retailing professional-grade cameras, photographic accessories, and supplies, as well as developing photos for amateur shutterbugs. The 8mm home movie phenomenon was coming into vogue around the time Mel's opened, so the store stocked items for that market as well.

Mel Price's usual facial expression might have been dour, but he was enthusiastically involved with the Normandale Merchants' Association and served as its first secretary. Other merchants said the biggest smile they had ever seen on Price's face was during the previously noted 1955 visit to his store by actress Cleo Moore.

Some Normandale merchants' offspring got inspired by other businesses and pursued alternate careers from their parents. Barry Chrietzburg was a notable example—at an early age, he lost interest in hardware and became enamored with Mel's Photo Shop and the vast possibilities of photography. The younger Chrietzberg ultimately became an excellent photographer and opened a successful studio in Wetumpka.

THE NORMANDALE BAKERY OWNED and operated by Florence and Yancey Liger was hailed by many Montgomery residents as the best in the city. Established downtown in 1944, Liger's Bakery

*Liger's worker with one of the bakery's legendary cakes—PR.*

rye and pumpernickel. All of the recipes were original and were made with whole eggs, butter, milk, etc. Nothing was 'instant.'"

Among the favorite items at Liger's were thumbprint cookies, gingerbread men, cherry brandy walnut cake, cream horns, donuts, mint cookies, petit-fours, fudge brownies, sand tarts, and meringue pies (lemon, coconut, and chocolate).

"Birthday, wedding, and all-occasion cakes were also very popular," Radford remarked. "We always had a team of decorators, including my granddad's sister, Aunt Belle. I spent many an hour during my youth watching them crank out works of art."

Radford accompanied his grandfather on a delivery in the mid-1960s to the Governor's Mansion on Perry Street, where he met then-Governor Lurleen Wallace. "I remember her as a very kind and gracious lady who treated my granddad like they were old friends," said Radford.

built its reputation by utilizing the finest quality ingredients. The Ligers' grandson, Tony Radford, worked in the bakery as a teenager He cited his grandfather's meticulous effort in baking perfect French bread:

"He was a quintessential perfectionist when it came to his craft. During a trip he and Granny made to New Orleans, they were amazed by the taste and texture of the bread served in the French Quarter. He went to great efforts to duplicate it at Liger's. But even after bringing back samples of their local water, he was never able to reproduce it to his satisfaction. Still, our original recipe of French bread was in high demand every day, as was our

Another thing he recalls was that his grandparents "established Liger's Bakery during a tough racial period in Alabama. Even the Loveman's department store, the main attraction at Normandale, had White and Colored drinking fountains. All of the bakers my granddad hired were young African-American men with no skills. He trained them personally—Homer, Lightning, Eddie. They were loyal and treasured members of the Liger's Bakery family for decades. Of course, they're all gone now, but I remember them well."

BY THE MIDDLE OF 1958, a new fabric store called The Yardstick was operating on the original front

*Bernie Gross—PR.*

Other Witt family members worked at Toyland, and Harry recalled the uniqueness of selling merchandise for a specific, much younger market to members of older generations that were doing the actual purchasing.

"In the minds of most people, a toy store was simply where you bought toys," he said, "and of course, Christmas was the busiest time for us; probably 60 to 70 percent of our business was done then. The rest of the year we were just treading water. It wasn't like today, where every Walmart has a toy department—that's because there weren't any Walmarts." Toyland also attracted many customers from surrounding towns and counties, particularly on weekends.

Harry recalled that the Toyland owners had to react quickly when items abruptly became national fads. He cited Hula Hoops (1958) and Chatty Cathy dolls (1960) as examples. The general layout for Toyland had displays of girls' items on one side of the store and boys' items on the other. Dolls were offered at various price points, including collectible Madame Alexander dolls.

Ready-to-assemble model airplanes and car kits from companies like AMF, Revell, and Monogram were popular. Toyland would regularly schedule model car contests for young customers. Many entries were highly customized and featured spectacular finishes. Some would be displayed in Toyland's front window. The competitions were so popular that F. W. Woolworth, located across the arcade, also began staging model car contests.

Harry emphasized that Toyland sold more than fantasy/escapist merchandise. "We advertised that we had a 'science department' with microscopes, telescopes. Items designed to stimulate your education."

line. Its proprietors were Iyla and Bernard Gross. Bernie was originally from Cleveland and had worked in department stores in other states before opening his own "fashion fabric" store in Montgomery. The Grosses immediately became active in the Normandale Merchants' Association.

TOYLAND IN NORMANDALE WAS originally owned by a young businessman named Lionel Gordon. His associate, Bennie Witt, became a partner when the business opened a second store in the Forest Hills Shopping Center. Witt became the owner of both stores by around 1960, according to Witt's son, Harry, who began working in the business when he was ten years old.

"In the early days, he bought everything from a wholesale jobber," Harry recounted. "Dexter Toyland downtown was run by different people, but they would work together and come up with ways to buy a whole truckload of things like Tonka trucks."

Witt said that as with many Normandale retailers, service played a big part in Toyland's success. "We would put bicycles together for you. We delivered them to your house. People didn't have SUVs back then. We put swing sets together in customers' back yards."

Harry's childhood memories of the shopping center extended beyond his family's business. He acknowledged the attraction of Santa upstairs in the Loveman's display window. And, "for me, it was Liger's. Absolutely the best bakery I've ever been to in my life."

WITH ALL DUE RESPECT to the photographic efforts of Paul Robertson and John Engelhardt Scott, Normandale had a photography studio as a tenant, owned and operated by Herb Yutmeyer. The studio was tucked away in the short "spur" of businesses lined up behind Loveman's southwest side (one Yutmeyer ad described the location as "Set Back of Loveman's").

Yutmeyer's business was oriented more toward heavy oil portraits than commercial photography. He was a native of Cincinnati and was operating a small facility in downtown Opelika when the Normandale opportunity came along in 1956.

Herb's wife Grace was an "artistic assistant" with the business, applying oil paint to photographs to convert the images to oil portraits. They won numerous awards, and some of their work was exhibited in New York City. Other portraits were displayed at the Alabama Governor's Mansion.

Yutmeyer was an enthusiastic handball player and could often be found during his time off on one of the courts in the downtown YMCA. He was a supporter of that organization for many years.

ANOTHER BUSINESS TUCKED AWAY behind Loveman's was Mark Hall, a card and gift store operated by Henry Greenfield and his wife. The shop was promoted as filling a retail niche for greeting cards, inexpensive gifts, party goods and gag gifts.

IF EVER A POLL had been taken regarding the most iconic retail personality in the history of Normandale, the winner would probably have been Raymond Cohen, proprietor of the Record Shop.

The perpetually upbeat store owner began his sales career with his older brother, Isaac, at the family-owned Cohen Amusement Company, located on Dexter Avenue downtown. Like Rubin Franco's family business, the Cohens maintained vending machines, arcade games, and jukeboxes around the Capital City.

The retailing of popular records was just developing in the early 1950s—45 rpm singles and 33⅓ rpm albums. Raymond and Isaac began selling records downtown, but separated their business in 1957. Raymond opted to move into the new expansion of the huge shopping center in south Montgomery.

Raymond's oldest son, Michael, recalled with a chuckle: "My dad and Aaron Aronov were buddies, and they may have leaned on each other."

The Record Shop's first location was 975 square feet of floor space in the short row of stores on the "spur" on the eastern side of the arcade. "I remember the original store being off to the side, behind Loveman's," said Michael. "One of the stores next to ours moved out, so Dad got that space too, and knocked out the wall."

∾

*Singer and songwriter Toni Wood recalls that "I was one of those kids that lived in the neighborhood behind Normandale. My first 'big girl' bicycle was purchased at Western Auto. That gave me freedom to go to Normandale anytime I wanted to. I would save my lunch money so I could go to Woolworth's for a banana split! And then, Raymond Cohen opened The*

*Record Shop, my home away from home. I was there so much, he said he should hire me. He had booths you could go into and listen on headphones to a record before you bought it. My lunch money was now being saved for the latest 45! I had to have the latest releases! I pestered him daily and would wait for the delivery truck. My mother would call there looking for me. Mr. Cohen would say, that was your mother, you've got to go home. He was always kind and tolerant of me."*

COHEN ALSO COLLABORATED WITH a local radio station to broadcast new albums over the airwaves during programs advertised in the newspaper as "Symphony in Hi-Fi over WHHY — Tonight — The Record Shop, Normandale Arcade."

The Record Shop had every intention of living up to its moniker, but to say the business "expanded" or "diversified" is an understatement. Cohen began to get calls for audio products including record

*Isaac and Raymond Cohen with a new cigarette vending machine, 1957—ADAH.*

players and reel-to-reel tape players, so he began selling those items. That additional merchandise category was ultimately followed by televisions and audio gear for new music formats like 8-track and cassette tapes. Raymond always recalled that his business was lucky to have been established by the time the American consumer audio-visual market rapidly evolved into a massive phenomenon.

As the new concept of two-speaker stereophonic sound entered the marketplace, the Record Shop offered high-fidelity components for customers who wanted to design their own home sound systems. Raymond developed retail accounts with customers who would use his store's branded credit cards. He even offered charge accounts to teenagers.

"That was back when your word meant something," said Michael. "I think he got a lot of business because he carried his own accounts, and that lasted until sometime in the 1980s. I hear those stories a lot from many customers who appreciated what a great gesture that was."

Montgomery native and businessman Roger Tyus was an example of Raymond's customers who had started doing business with the Record Shop at an early age, utilizing an in-store charge account—when Tyus was too young to have a driver's license.

"I had been buying eight-tracks and vinyl [LPs] from the Record Shop," Roger remembered, "so Mr. Cohen knew me. I wanted an eight-track player for my home; I was maybe fourteen years old and was still cutting grass to earn money. Mr. Cohen had always been cordial, and he offered to set me up with my own account, *at my age*. I filled out a credit application and never had any problems. He was the first person to offer me a charge account, and it went on for decades. He couldn't have been more courteous."

Not surprisingly, the Record Shop also outgrew its space behind Loveman's and moved into

*Raymond Cohen—courtesy of Cohen's.*

the store formerly occupied by Thom McAn in the main arcade. A primary reason the business moved to a larger store was the evolution of television sets—sometimes accompanied by record players—being retailed as "consoles"; i.e., pieces of furniture that housed electronic entertainment equipment.

"When we moved around the corner, we had two big glass windows to showcase whatever we wanted," Michael said, "but when you got inside, there were all kinds of 25-inch console TVs in all kinds of furniture styles—Spanish black oak, Early American maple, French Provincial with the four legs, others."

The younger Cohen also noted that in the Record Shop's earlier days television dealers could offer cash discounts to customers. "These days, with everything so commoditized, you're lucky if you can break even on TVs, particularly if somebody gives you a modern-day type of credit card."

The Record Shop continued to diversify, enhancing its reputation with mid-1970s innovations for home entertainment and convenience such as Sony Betamax video recorders and Amana Radar Range microwave ovens. Higher-end audio components included brands such as Marantz, Fisher, Bose, Klipsch, JBL, and Sansui. Nevertheless, the larger store had a larger record department and was one of the few area stores with a large selection of classical/symphonic albums. A service department and small warehouse were added to the layout of the larger arcade store.

"At one point, we were using one of my grandfather's apartments to store console TVs," Michael recalled.

UNDER THE AEGIS OF Bill Denson, promotions were rolling along on a regular basis, including contests like "Strike It Rich" and "Wheel of Fortune."

An annual Easter promotion was introduced in March 1958 as the shopping center's "Giant

*1958 Normandale
ads included one at
left for an Easter
event and the one
above for a June
cooking contest.
At far left, the
list of cooks and
their Normandale
merchant sponsors.*

*Above, an Air Force family peruses merchandise in an "Easy Living" promotion. The captain's shorts and long socks were an authorized uniform during a brief USAF experiment. Above right, the same family tries out the still-unique escalators in Loveman's. Below, an Air Force major and his wife examine new window-mount air conditioners at Loveman's. —PR.*

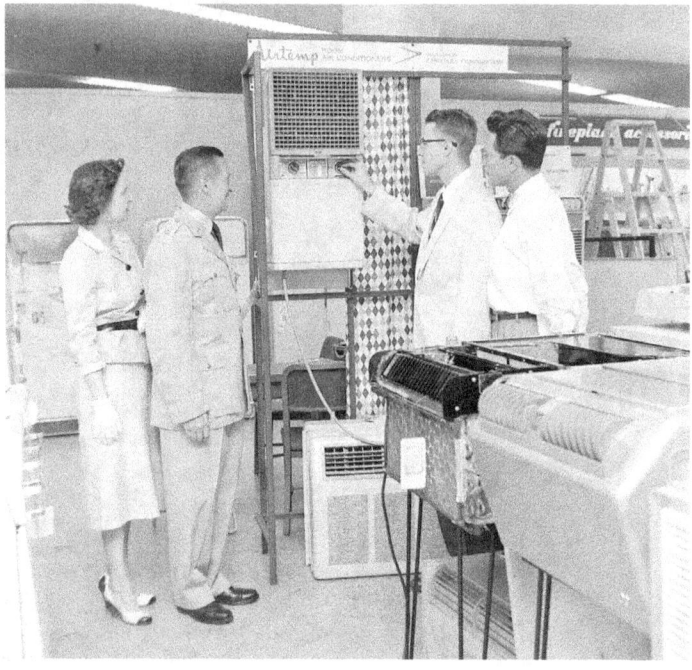

Easter Bunnies," Norman and Dale, roamed the walkways and dispensed "free candy & favors" to youngsters.

Normandale's first ambitious *Redbook* "Easy Living" event was staged May 1–15, 1958. It was inspired by a feature in the longtime women's magazine (a Hearst publication), and Normandale was one of forty shopping centers nationwide selected for the event. The local presentation included dog and fashion shows, a concert by the Cloverdale Junior High School band, a dance contest, a boat and motor show, and an automobile show that included station wagons, Corvettes, and house trailers.

Capitol Chevrolet set up a $250,000

"Featurama" exhibit, a widely acclaimed presentation that demonstrated mechanical principles of General Motors products. Mayor Gayle issued a "Whereas" proclamation to mark the event.

Other 1958 Normandale promotions included an outdoor cooking contest in late June (Paul Robertson and Joe Azbell were among the contestants), as well as special sales like "Bargain Days" and "Back To School."

NORMANDALE MERCHANTS WERE KEENLY aware of the retail sales potential of United States Air Force personnel and their families who were stationed in Montgomery. The growth of Maxwell Air Force Base by the Alabama River, as well as Gunter Air Force Base on the city's northeast side, annually brought in hundreds of airmen and their dependents, and retailers endeavored to offer the type of merchandise that would appeal to families with a transient lifestyle.

A photograph of a line of C-97 aircraft on the tarmac at Maxwell Air Force Base (courtesy of James Scott) was among the gigantic local scenery murals displayed at the entrance to Kwik Chek. As would be the scenario at Robert Kennedy's speech at the Whitley Hotel a few years later, John Engelhardt Scott had taken the original photos that ended up as murals in Kwik Chek, and he later photographed the interior entrance of the grocery store, where the murals were displayed (courtesy of ADAH).

MANY OUT-OF-TOWN CUSTOMERS TREKKED to sprawling Normandale to take advantage of its huge selection of merchandise. Ellen Williams recalls that her in-laws Steve and Vestera Williams, farmers in the Marcoot community of Chambers County, used to drive their Ford pick-up the eighty-five miles south to Normandale to take in the variety of stores and look for bargains for their large family. Shoppers from towns like Wetumpka

and Tallassee, northeast of the Capital City, might be more oriented towards Eastbrook and Forest Hills shopping centers because they were closer by. Yet even families from those communities would bypass the smaller eastside shopping centers to patronize Normandale.

"We would come down to Montgomery on Highway 231," Tallassee resident Tommy Mann recalled. "This was before the interstate highway was built, and the first red light on our trips was at the intersection by Capitol Heights Junior High School. We'd make a right, then a quick left onto Ann Street, working our way over to Normandale, which was really the first place we knew of that was called a 'shopping center.' That was really a new term back then."

As a young boy residing in a small mill town like Tallassee, Mann developed an early interest in automobiles and looked forward to trips to Normandale's Western Auto and Parker-Sledge Hardware stores. "Those stores in Normandale carried stuff that I'd never seen," Mann recalled.

His family trips to Normandale usually included dining at the Francis Cafeteria.

And like children who were Montgomery residents, the youngsters from out of town were always fascinated by the shopping center's voluminous Christmas decorations and displays, and, of course, Santa Claus. Mann: "We had a Santa Claus in Tallassee, but I remember how impressive the Santa at Normandale was, sitting in that big window upstairs at Loveman's."

❧

*Tommy Mann would later become the lead singer for a popular pop/rock band called the K-Otics, who duked it out nationally with another band, the Swingin' Medallions, on competing versions of a song called "Double Shot." The K-Otics appeared at one of Montgomery's fabled "Big Bam Shows," sponsored by WBAM Radio and staged at the Coliseum. Other artists appearing at the same caravan-style concert included the Lovin' Spoonful, Peter and Gordon, and heartthrob Lou Christie.*

"WE SHOPPED AT EASTBROOK," Alexander City resident Steve Forehand said of his family's sojourns to Montgomery, "but we liked Normandale because it was larger, and it seemed to have more of the stores we liked. We also liked the Christmas decorations;

our trips to Normandale were primarily Christmas-oriented. We had Frohsin's and the Fair Store here (in Alexander City) for back-to-school clothing.

"And I was always impressed with the neighborhoods around Normandale—how neat and well-maintained the yards were. It seemed like we always got there around dark, so the Christmas lights were sort of a beacon."

DON HEACOCK WAS RAISED in Uniontown, a small west Alabama town located between Selma and Demopolis on U.S. Highway 80. The number of stores and variety of merchandise at Normandale fascinated his entire family.

"We'd go to Selma for regular shopping at the stores downtown," he recalled, "but a trip to Normandale was like going to Disney World! We would usually go there for Christmas shopping, but I remember a couple of times where we just went on a whim.

"My mother preferred to shop at Loveman's instead of the other clothing stores, because she had shopped at the original Loveman's in downtown Birmingham, starting in 1944. She had worked as a secretary for Tennessee Coal and Iron—which became part of U.S. Steel—in the Brown-Marx Building. But another appealing part of Loveman's back then was the new business of men's fragrances. Stores moved beyond Aqua Velva, Old Spice or [Mennen] Skin Bracer. Loveman's sold brands like English Leather and Russian Leather. Originally, British Sterling was only supposed to be available at jewelry stores, but I think it ended up in Loveman's, as well."

Other popular men's fragrances marketed by Loveman's included Jade East, Brut, Imperial Saber and the higher-priced Canoe.

A self-described "car nut" from a young age, Heacock, like Tommy Mann, obviously enjoyed visiting Normandale's large Western Auto store.

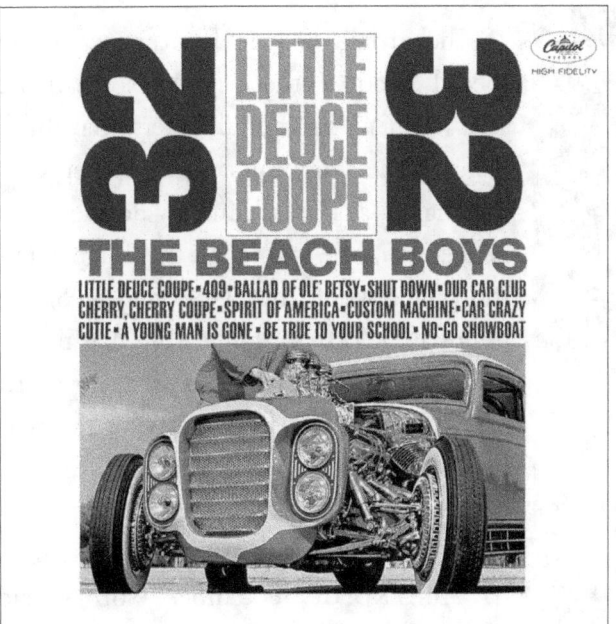

He also remembered an automotive connection to the Record Shop, which was going strong with its private listening cubicles. The youngster from west Alabama "desperately" coveted a Beach Boys album from late 1963, *Little Deuce Coupe,* but his parents wouldn't let him purchase it.

The Heacocks tried to patronize a favorite restaurant whenever they came to the Capital City to shop at Normandale, but it wasn't the Francis Cafeteria. "We preferred the Ranch restaurant," Don recalled, "out on the corner of Mobile Highway and Air Base Boulevard, near Maxwell Air Force Base. Later, we would dine at the Elite Café in downtown Montgomery."

When he was a cadet at Marion Military Institute (also in west Alabama), Heacock's activities included work with the school's journalism projects. He and a friend from Notasulga co-edited two yearbooks, and they would journey east on Highway 80 to buy photographic supplies from Mel's Photo Shop in Normandale.

As usual, the front page of the now-expected special newspaper section created for Normandale's fourth anniversary had a plethora of positive

articles with upbeat titles—"During '58, Normandale Becomes Shopping CITY (sic)," "Normandale's Beauty Grows Under Organized Programs," "No More Parking Problems," "Center Fulfills Hopes Held by Aaron Aronov," "Auditorium Set for Meetings at Normandale," "Suburban Living Reflected," "Merchants Association Looks to Convenience of Shoppers."

In particular, the Aronov profile was appropriate, as the business magnate, who was still developing numerous other projects, ruminated on what Normandale had accomplished so far, as well as plans for the future.

One popular promotion that was presented in sync with the fourth anniversary was a series of "Bonus Bucks" auctions. For a specific length of time, shoppers were presented with Normandale "bonus bucks" rated at five times the amount of

*This "Bonus Bucks" auction session was covered by WSFA-TV—PR.*

The article on the front page of the special section that cited Normandale as a "CITY" in capital letters may have inspired the shopping center's owners and merchants, as they ultimately decided that henceforth, the name of the huge retail showplace would be "Normandale Shopping City." A large sign bearing that moniker would later be installed on the western edge of Normandale's property by Norman Bridge Road, near the People's Bank & Trust building.

AT THE END OF September, Normandale took advantage of a national fad to stage a hula hoop contest in the parking lot. Five categories were slated. The "endurance" competition was cancelled when darkness fell and a dozen contestants were still going strong.

their purchases. Such funny money could be used to bid on items during the evening auctions, which were staged over several nights in a row during the anniversary. Among the merchandise were cameras, hi-fi consoles, furniture, grills, watches, and lawnmowers.

Some stores came up with their own unique promotions. Virginia Dare's "mutt contest" was a definitive example (Paul Robertson photo, below).

In late 1958, the Montgomery Little Theater organization acquired a deconsecrated church building on Goldthwaite Street near downtown Montgomery. The organization moved to that location the following year, but on more than one occasion the troupe returned to its old haunts underneath the W. T. Grant store.

In spite of the overall rousing success of Normandale's merchants, some stores struggled. When Pauline Wilkins Candies departed its small

space next to Loveman's late in the decade, an ambitious recent Auburn University graduate in his early twenties named Dick McAdams opened a carpet company in that location.

"It was only one thousand square feet," he recalled. The new merchant quickly loaded up his literally small business with carpet samples. The minimal floor space served McAdams well, since he was exhibiting only small pieces of his wares for customers to examine. McAdams Carpets received an award in a national shopping center contest for the highest-dollar-amount-of-sales-per-square-foot, having been boosted for the citation by the Normandale Merchants' Association.

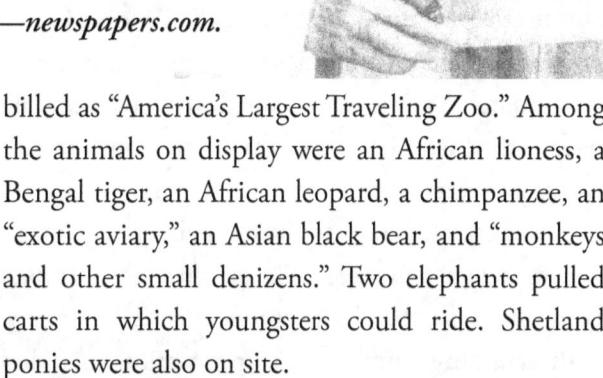

*Left, Meredith Harrell. Right, Lieutenant Governor Boutwell on the phone to Hawaii—newspapers.com.*

BY 1958, NORMANDALE WAS stable and prospering. Droves of customers came from all directions, retailers experienced phenomenal sales, and frequently staged promotions pleased the crowds. Everyday business was voluminous, and customers quickly came to expect quality merchandise at fair prices.

Montgomery native Meredith Harrell, who had previously worked for the *Montgomery Advertiser* and the *Alabama Journal,* replaced Bill Denson as the executive secretary of the Normandale Merchants' Association in early 1959. His tenure would last more than twenty years. Harrell formed a close friendship with fellow dynamo Raymond Cohen and met often with the Record Shop owner to discuss improvements to Normandale's structure and operation.

Unique promotional events for Harrell's first year included the April appearance of Animaland, billed as "America's Largest Traveling Zoo." Among the animals on display were an African lioness, a Bengal tiger, an African leopard, a chimpanzee, an "exotic aviary," an Asian black bear, and "monkeys and other small denizens." Two elephants pulled carts in which youngsters could ride. Shetland ponies were also on site.

"What Meredith Harrell did regarding promotions for Normandale was extraordinary," Owen Aronov enthused. "He was great at organizing events sponsored by the Merchants' Association. And we could do things back then that we can't do now—elephants in the parking lot, for example."

In June, Harrell supervised two promotions that were as clever and innovative as anything his predecessors had done.

Hawaii was about to become the nation's fiftieth state, and as part of a "Welcome Hawaii, the 50th Star" promotion, Harrell arranged a long distance phone call between Hawaii governor William Quinn and Alabama lieutenant governor Albert Boutwell on Friday, June 5. The conversation was broadcast through the shopping center's built-in sound system for the benefit of customers on the premises.

Also attending the unique event were two U.S. Air Force airmen—both of whom happened to be women. Rita M. Pico and Harriet Jones were native Hawaiians assigned to Maxwell Air Force Base.

Other Hawaii-oriented facets of the promotion included palm trees and decorations throughout the arcade. The Loree Atkins School of Dance presented a variety dance show on June 4.

The same day as the Boutwell phone call to Hawaii, Normandale looked across the Atlantic Ocean as well, teaming up with the local Renault automobile dealership, the C. E. Pitts Motor Company, and Foremost Dairies to promote the latter's new French Vanilla ice cream flavor. Normandale had worked with the Pitts firm on previous promotional projects, as noted in Chapter 6.

The Renault Dauphine was a small, French-made automobile that was, in those times, a legitimate competitor to the Volkswagen "Beetle" as a no-frills economy nimport. The promotion included the display of a two-and-a-half story inflatable in the shape of an ice cream container, surrounded by Dauphines. A live broadcast on WCOV Radio was done from the top of the "container," which was, naturally, proclaimed to be the "world's tallest ice cream carton."

HARRELL'S RELENTLESS PACE CONTINUED through the summer. Mid-July saw one of the most unique promotions ever staged at Normandale, as an igloo—yes, made of ice—was constructed on the premises. It was monitored closely by customers and merchants as it melted. Prizes were awarded to registered entrants who had guessed closest to the exact time the igloo would turn completely from a solid into a liquid. This promotion was

*Top, the giant Foremost ice cream carton, encircled by Renault automobiles (eight Eight Dauphines were given away in the promotion) —ADAH.*

*Above, depicted in a press release, the igloo was well on its way to a watery demise when this photo was taken. Right, other 1958 ads for the center.*

sponsored by the *Montgomery Advertiser* and the *Alabama Journal.*

Normandale's fifth anniversary was celebrated in August instead of September and included a contingent of Seminoles performing native dances. Another five hundred pound cake was baked (albeit by Cosby Hodges Milling Company, makers of White Tulip flour), and Mayor Gayle visited the shopping center to help serve it to customers.

Among the public relations articles in the local newspaper during the fifth anniversary was a citation of DeShields-Larson Shoes manager Letha Watson, who had worked every shopping evening since the store had opened five years earlier. Concerts by the Robert E. Lee High School band and the Jim Russell Band were also noted. The inclusion of the Lee band intimated that Normandale

was continuing its efforts to extend its influence into the northeast section of Montgomery.

THE SPECIAL CHRISTMAS PROMOTION for 1959 was an ambitious "Never-Never Land" display, populated by Mother Goose characters. New Montgomery mayor Earl James and Santa officially opened the exhibit of custom-crafted, larger-than-life figures from nursery rhymes.

An interesting bit of visual irony was seen during at least one Christmas season, and one wonders whether the alignment of the display was intentional. Lighted decorations that were placed over the Western Auto store showed the silhouettes of a camel between two human figures with walking staffs. To most observers, the figures would probably have represented two of the three Wise Men from traditional Christian Scripture . . . which meant that the figures were placed in a direction that matched the Bible story—"Wise Men from the East" on a journey in a westerly direction, above a *Western* Auto store on the west-facing side of Normandale's front line of stores (Paul Robertson photo, below).

# 10

# The Early 1960s — Banana Bicycle Seats, Banana Splits, and 'Backwards Flip' Commode Seats—

The decade of the 1960s saw Normandale settling into its status as an iconic shopping mecca. Local families as well as out-of-towners counted on Normandale for almost any type of merchandise, and its gargantuan, constantly evolving "shopping city" concept continued to enhance its legend and mystique.

THE DISPLAYS AT LOVEMAN'S presented clothing and fashion accessories (including fragrances) on the bottom floor, and furniture, appliances, electronics, books, and more on the second floor.

"Their record department was wonderful!" recalled William "Sonny" Bozeman, a retired college professor who played in Montgomery bands starting in his teens. "They had several turntables and you could listen to albums. The manager of the department was reported to be the sister of WHHY radio deejay Bill O'Brien, a *huge* figure in local pop music in the late 1950s. He hosted a long nightly show called 'Night Train'; the theme song was Buddy Morrow's classic recording. Later

in the evening he had a second program, 'Music for Lovers Only.' I recall my mom telling me to turn off my radio and go to sleep when that show came on! He also hosted the Saturday morning 'Teen Time' stage show at the Paramount Theatre that was broadcast live on WHHY."

AT THE ADVENT OF the Sixties, the F. W. Woolworth retail chain had approximately 2,500 stores in North America and more than 1,000 stores in Great Britain. The W. T. Grant chain had almost 1,200 stores at its peak.

The Woolworth's in the rear of the Normandale arcade was situated next to the W. T. Grant store, with the main entrances at right angles to each other. Their proximity meant that customers often shopped one then the other.

Indeed, there were obvious similarities—both stores sold "general merchandise," including sundries, notions and household items, but the larger W. T. Grant stores were hyped as having a "junior department store" concept with a wider selection of merchandise. The terms "variety store" and "self-service" were also applied to the W. T. Grant marketing strategy.

Woolworth's merchandise was perceived as slightly more budget-oriented, which is why, to many shoppers, "five-and-dime store" and similar idioms would probably have been used to describe Woolworth's rather than Grant's.

Some items sold at Grant's and Woolworth's were faddish. For example, among the small indoor pets sold by both stores were baby turtles, often sporting painted shells. The species was known as the red-eared slider (*Trachemys scripta elegans*). The painted shell trend didn't last long, and the same could be said for the decorated turtles themselves.

Both stores sold records and record players, but Grant's also marketed major appliances and television sets—another facet of the "junior department store" strategy. The house brand for Grant's electronics and appliances was Bradford; Woolworth's house brand for its audio items was Audition. And when the Beatles appeared on the *Ed Sullivan Show* in February 1964, the "'60s guitar boom" that resulted meant that Bradford and Audition house

*Electric guitars sold by Woolworth's, Grant's, and Western Auto: from top, Bradford; Audition; both imaged by HA.com;*

*Truetone solidbody — Bill Ingalls Jr.; and Truetone thinline —Wikimedia Commons.*

*Top, this display in Woolworth's included Timex watches and Norbee pendant watches. Bottom, "flip-flops" at a whopping 69 cents a pair. —PR.*

brand guitars appeared in their respective stores.

The same type of in-house branding could also be found at Western Auto, on the original front line of Normandale by Lee's Drugs. That store's house brand for its televisions and audio merchandise (including guitars) was Truetone.

THE ORIGINAL RESTROOMS AT W. T. Grant in Normandale were unique for more than one reason. First, they were still pay toilets at a time when charging admission to a water closet was beginning to fade away in America. Secondly, the seats of the commodes were spring-mounted. When a customer wasn't seated, the seat was stored upright inside a housing with an ultraviolet light system to kill germs. The seat had to be pulled down manually, but would automatically flip backwards into its housing when the user stood up. This created more than one potentially awkward scenario, and such toilets were eventually replaced. Lastly, the restrooms were racially segregated.

~

*South Montgomery raconteur Tom McCabe, who was an active member of the Montgomery Little Theater, recalled that the last retail business in Montgomery that had been built with separate toilets and water fountains was the Sears store on the corner of Court Street and Fairview Avenue, near Sidney Lanier High School. Sears moved from downtown Montgomery to the new store in 1963.*

ONE OBVIOUS PLUS FOR Woolworth's was its lengthy luncheonette counter, offering cheap food at cheap prices. One 1960s teenager recalled occasionally dining on canned chili con carne at

Paul Robertson

Woolworth's. While its taste was palatable—at least, to her—the contents didn't look too appetizing, so she crumbled up crackers and stirred them into the bowl as sort of a disguise for her meal.

1960 happened to be an important annum for Woolworth's lunch counters for two memorable reasons—one historical, one whimsical and more egalitarian.

On February 1, 1960, four black college students attempted to dine at a Woolworth's lunch counter in Greensboro, North Carolina. When refused service, they declined to leave and were arrested. The subsequent peaceful sit-in movement spread quickly across the South and was among the earlier nonviolent protests of the civil rights era.

As noted in Chapter 1, Normandale had opened some fifteen months before Rosa Parks's arrest in downtown Montgomery. Although the new shopping center had "colored" customers, many, if not most of the stores still had segregated toilets and/or water fountains. At least one business had segregated waiting rooms.

And after the Civil Rights Act of 1964 was signed into law, some white Montgomerians engaged in speculation and rumor mongering as to where and when Negro activists would test the new law locally. The Woolworth's luncheonette in Normandale might have seemed like an appropriate location, but if any action was planned, it apparently wasn't publicized, before or after.

∽

*Not long after the Civil Rights Act of 1964 became law, this writer, then fourteen years old, ordered a chocolate malt at the Woolworth's luncheonette in Normandale and began slurping on it while seated. It was then that I noticed a solitary black female dining further down the row of seats. She apparently finished while I was still enjoying my malt, as she paid for her order and left without incident.*

*And that's all there was to it. I remember thinking to myself, "What's the big deal?"*

THE OTHER MEMORABLE 1960 occurrence involving the F. W. Woolworth chain wasn't particularly historic, but it was fun—that was the year the company introduced its "Pick-A-Balloon" promotion in all its stores nationally. At the time, the luncheonette's Super Jumbo banana split (with "3 large dips of ice cream") cost 39 cents. The dining areas of Woolworth's stores were decorated with balloons containing slips of paper numbered from 1 to 39, which was the amount the customer would pay for his/her treat after popping the balloon. Some tags were labeled "Free."

"Seemed like all the ones I popped had a tag inside that said '39'," one former customer grumbled good-naturedly years later. Rigged or not, the promotion was popular and was presented for many years, even as the price of Super Jumbo banana splits increased.

SUPER JUMBO
**BANANA SPLIT**
3 LARGE DIPS OF ICE CREAM ON BANANA TOPPED WITH
YOUR FAVORITE FLAVOR, WHIPPED TOPPING AND ROASTED NUTS
**39¢**
F.W. WOOLWORTH CO.

MEREDITH HARRELL EXCELLED as Normandale's head promoter for the entire decade and beyond, pumping out press releases and staging hyped-up presentations on a regular basis.

In March 1960, Normandale was one of fifty shopping centers participating in another *Redbook*-sponsored "Easy Living" promotion. This time around, a national contest for young families figured into the mix, and the grand prize was an all-expenses-paid family vacation to Scandinavia on Icelandic Airlines. Many of the demonstrations and displays from the 1958 event at Normandale were updated and presented again. There was also a model airplane contest and a trailer show. The promotion lasted nine days and, like the 1958 event,

*Loveman's employees dressed for comfort at a Come-As-You-Are/Casual Wednesday—PR.*

was officially proclaimed in a "Whereas" document by new Montgomery Mayor Earl James (he served from 1959 through 1971).

Lou Herman, then-president of the Normandale Merchants Association, welcomed two *Redbook* corporate officials to Montgomery during the event.

IN EARLY MAY 1960, Normandale shoppers probably thought that March's "Easy Living" promotion had carried over to the historic Ford/Chevrolet competition when Ford's "Design for Station Wagon Living" exhibition made a solo appearance.

Ford had been pushing the mobility-livability concept of station wagons for several years. In 1957, the company published a 256-page book, *The Ford Treasury of Station Wagon Living*, sized to fit into an automobile's glove compartment.

The traveling exhibition that

FORD TREASURY OF
# Station Wagon Living

A GUIDE TO OUTDOOR RECREATION, WITH A DIRECTORY OF OVER 1300 CAMPGROUNDS AND FIELD TEST REPORTS ON 140 ITEMS OF CAMP GEAR

---

The Time:
**JULY 1–JULY 9**
The Place:
NORMANDALE SHOPPING CENTER
The Performance:

# THE CHEVY CINESPHERE

It's astonishing! Incredible! An entirely new experience in motion picture realism! You watch Cinesphere and suddenly you're part of it, actually experiencing its thrills and excitement. Don't miss it for the world! At the same time you'll see a bright-shiny array of new Chevrolet cars and trucks, and a number of fascinating displays. A treat for the whole family. Plan to see Cinesphere today!

CHEVROLET

See the Cinesphere – a unique movie house and auditorium which inflates from a 4-ft. x 4-ft. package in a full-size building (approximately two stories high) in a matter of minutes.

WIN A FREE MINIATURE CORVETTE

## YOU'VE NEVER SEEN A SHOW LIKE THIS ONE!
DON'T MISS THE EXCITING CHEVROLET CINESPHERE SHOW
NORMANDALE SHOPPING CENTER, THROUGH JULY 9

---

made a stop in Normandale in 1960 featured displays of new camping, fishing, and hunting equipment alongside the "Push Button Camper," a station wagon that could be set up as a complete campsite with . . . well, the push of a button.

Chevrolet countered with a July exhibition of a new cinematic experience in an inflatable air-conditioned "theater," the Cine Sphere. The event was a collaboration between Normandale and Capitol Chevrolet, the local dealership. The innovative visual effects were somewhat like later movie formats such as Cinerama and IMAX. A local would-be wit opined that the

*Rosemary Murphy, Mrs. America 1961—Wikimedia Commons.*

exterior of the portable theater looked like a giant patty pan squash.

THE THEME FOR NORMANDALE'S 1960 birthday celebration was "We're Six in '60." The grand prize in an early September drawing was a 1960 Fiat automobile.

One unusual "prize" in a drawing sponsored by Lee's Drugs was free refills on prescriptions for a full year.

That fall, Normandale hosted a visit by Rosemary Murphy, the recently crowned Mrs. America for 1961. She attended a fashion show and was interviewed by local television show hostess Idelle Brooks. Murphy was from Kentland,

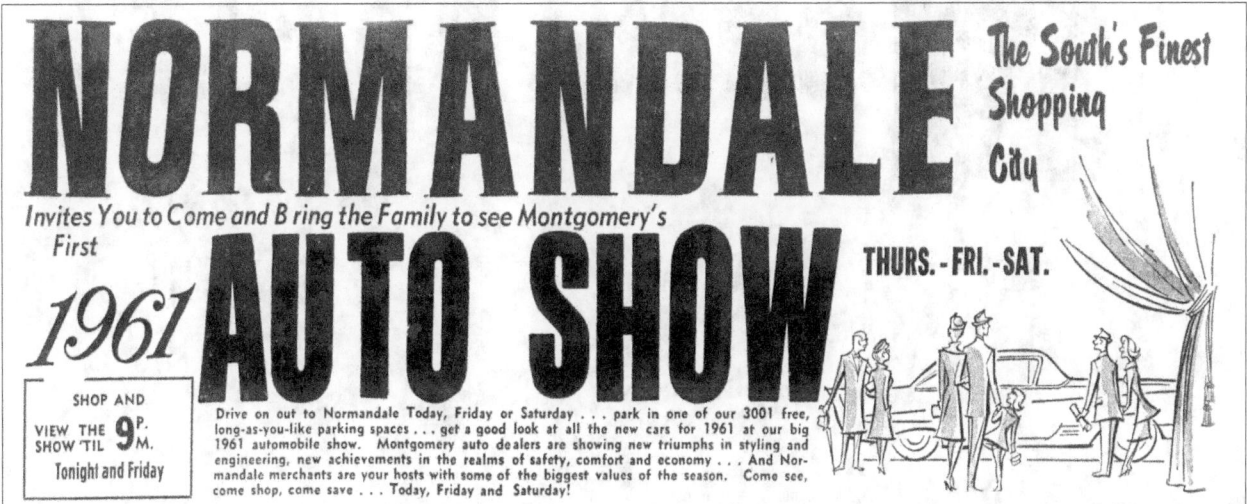

Indiana, and while her appearance didn't have the impact of the 1957 visit by then-Miss America Marian McKnight, it still added prestige and recognition to the shopping center.

In mid-November, Normandale collaborated with local automobile dealerships for an auto show.

THE 1961 CIVIL WAR centennial was a multi-faceted commemoration in Montgomery in February. Numerous events marked the hundred-year anniversary of the first capital of the Confederacy, including parades, formal balls, and the presentation of a play, *The Man and The Hour,* at the State Coliseum.

Men were encouraged to grow beards

*Above, Angel Gaddis, manager of the Loveman's toy department, conforms to the 1961 Civil War Centennial fashion guidelines by sporting a beard and a "Kentucky Colonel"-style tie—ADAH. Left, the City of Montgomery issued a commemorative CSA coin and made it legal tender locally.*

and some people dressed in period clothing for the week-long commemoration.

Research indicates that officially Normandale barely participated in Civil War Centennial events. A women's planning meeting was held in the community center in early January, and the same facility hosted a "Salute to the South" cooking school on Thursday, February 16, featuring 1,860 recipes. It was sponsored by Alabama Gas Company.

The next day, the final judging of the "Confederate Colonels Beard Contest" was held at Normandale.

The Montgomery population in 1961 was 38 percent black. Research was essentially silent on how African-Americans responded to the centennial.

TYPICAL OF MANY OF the local presentations at Normandale in that era was the Billy Pinkston Dance Studio's "Carnival of Dancing," an outdoor recital, in the front parking area on June 2, 1961.

For those shoppers who couldn't relate to dancing, a "collector's show" was staged in the community center. Sponsored by the Montgomery Area Safety Council, it was touted as "an outstanding exhibition of Montgomery's most unusual hobbies and crafts."

A July 1961 charity promotion that benefited the local United Appeal was, as advertised, "another first for Normandale." A large portable water tank was set up in the rear parking lot near Woolworth's and Grant's and was stocked with several hundred rainbow trout. Customers were provided with tackle and lures. Admission was 50 cents for adults and 25 cents for children.

NEW NORMANDALE TENANTS ARRIVING in the fall of 1961 included a branch of Investors Federal Savings and Loan

(opened August 1), an A&P grocery store (opened September 12), and a Gulf service station (opened in mid-September). The Gulf station, on the front

ADAH

edge of the parking lot on Patton Avenue across from LeBron Road, was hyped as a full-service facility offering repairs and tires, with uniformed attendants to pump gas.

The new A&P store next to W. T. Grant in the rear of the arcade ended Kwik Chek's monopoly as Normandale's only grocery store. The A&P construction began on March 20. At 16,800 square feet, it was the largest of seven A&P groceries in Montgomery, and it was the last original retail structure constructed at Normandale.

Kwik Chek, meanwhile, continued to perform strongly. In addition to its unusual exterior and giant mural photographs, Kwik Chek had begun building innovative and intricate displays of merchandise—particularly in the produce section—that would be part of the attraction for customers for years.

*Apple display inside Kwik Chek—ADAH.*

*Below, aerial view of Normandale with the A&P grocery addition, in the upper right corner in this photo from the Sidney Lanier High School* Oracle.

THE NEW STORE OPENINGS tied into the shopping city's "Lucky 7th" birthday promotion that was initiated in late August. The grand prize for a drawing

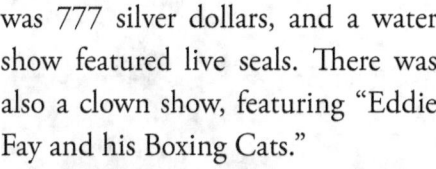

## NORMANDALE'S LUCKY 7th ANNIVERSARY CELEBRATION

Get the family together . . . come out
and join the fun . . .

# free

. . . be sure you register for

## 777 SILVER DOLLARS

### PLUS MANY OTHER PRIZES

Just pick up your registration blank from any store in Normandale, fill it out and drop in the ticket container on the sidewalk. You don't have to buy anything to be eligible to win and you do not have to be present.

Bring The Youngsters To See The Fascinating

**SEAL WATER CIRCUS**

In our east parking lot by Woolworth and Grants. The youngsters will enjoy feeding the seals for 10c.

---

**DRAWING TO BE HELD SATURDAY, SEPTEMBER 2—6 P.M.**

## Hundreds of Outstanding Values In Every One Of Our 43 Modern Stores. Everything You Need For Yourself, Your Family and Your Home.

**SHOP MONDAYS, THURSDAYS AND FRIDAYS 10 A.M. UNTIL 9 P.M. SHOP TUESDAYS, WEDNESDAYS & SATURDAYS 10 A.M. UNTIL 5:45 P.M.**

Your Youngsters Will Love Seeing THE MONTGOMERY LITTLE THEATRE'S Performance of

## "THE RED SHOES"

in The Normandale Community Center

FRIDAY — 7:30 P.M.
SATURDAY—2:30 P.M.

Admission
35c

was 777 silver dollars, and a water show featured live seals. There was also a clown show, featuring "Eddie Fay and his Boxing Cats."

The Montgomery Little Theater acting troupe temporarily relocated from Goldthwaite Street to the Normandale community center to stage a play for children, *The Red Shoes*.

Grant's used the occasion to announce a new policy of including S&H Green Stamps with purchases. Kwik Chek would later add the same bonus.

By late 1961, a movie theater-style marquee had been installed at the entrance to Normandale's breezeway.

LOVEMAN'S ACQUIRED A NEW store manager in July 1962 when Arthur Goodman, a branch manager at the Bessemer store, was transferred to Montgomery. Later in the decade, Arnold Unger assumed responsibilities as the Montgomery store manager.

Preliminary hype for the eighth birthday party in 1962 included a public relations article that hailed the celebration as an occurrence that would ". . . enhance Normandale's growing reputation as a cultural and entertainment center for Montgomery and central and south Alabama." The "star guest" for the occasion was Zippy the Chimp, who had appeared on *The Ed Sullivan Show, The Howdy*

*Zippy the Chimp—Wikimedia Commons.*

*Doody Show,* and *I've Got a Secret,* among other television broadcasts. The celebrity simian performed three times daily.

Decades later, a Montgomery curmudgeon who fancied himself a Deep South fine arts connoisseur would recall, "When that announcement used the word 'cultural,' I thought it meant they were gonna present something like a chamber music concert or maybe some ballet dancers. Then, here comes a monkey on roller skates. Jeezus . . ."

Grand prize for the expected drawing was 800 silver dollars, and store merchandise certificates were also awarded.

Citing the success of the presentation of *The Red Shoes* the previous year, the Montgomery Little Theater performed *Alice in Wonderland* in the community center during the birthday celebration.

In 1962, full-page composite advertising for Normandale stores still appeared in local newspapers. Some ads featured company names in their trademark logos, as seen on the adjacent Come-As-You-Are ad, while others had a cleaner, more

sophisticated look by using the same font for all merchants. Note the latter style on the 1962 Mother's Day ad (page 100).

WCOV's Walter Bamberg now had an alter ego, "Captain Zoomar," who hosted a weekday afternoon kiddie show broadcast live from the WCOV facilities on Adrian Lane, just a few blocks east of Normandale.

Each day, the live show featured a visiting group of youngsters (similar to *The Howdy Doody Show*'s "Peanut Gallery"), to whom the space captain would dutifully distribute small sample loaves of Holsum bread (in bright orange wrappers), as well as Classics Illustrated graphic novels (but "graphic novel" didn't exist as a term back then for the comic book-style adaptations of works by Charles Dickens, Victor Hugo, Jack London, Jules Verne, H. G. Wells, and others).

*Captain Zoomar and crew member Saturna (portrayed by Gloria Dodson) on the set of the WCOV-TV show—courtesy of David Bamberg.*

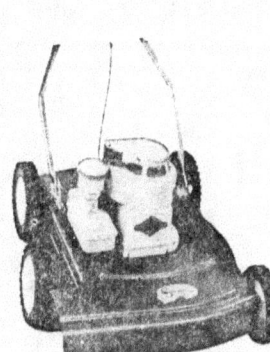

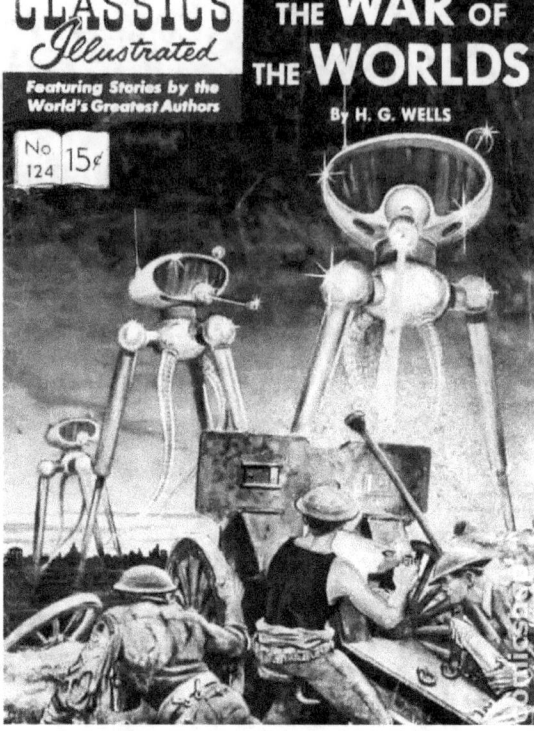
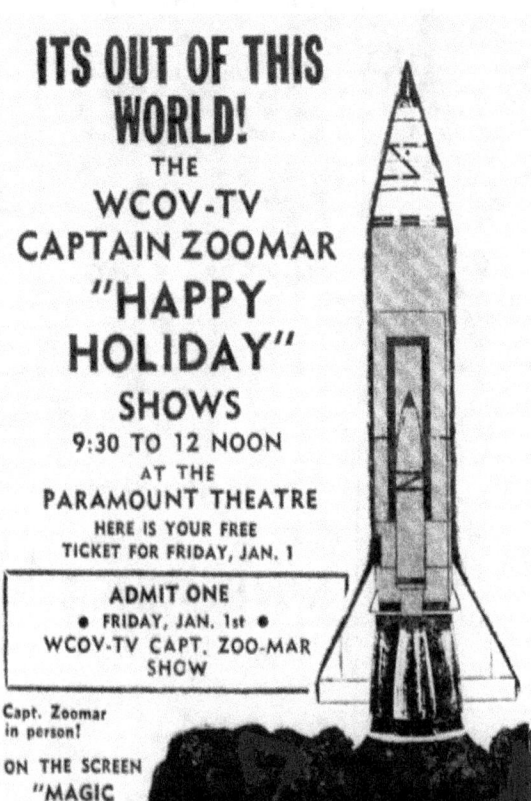

There was even a "Captain Zoomar Space Cadet Club." Each member received a signed certificate that intoned: "This is to certify that [child's name] is a qualified Channel 20 Space Cadet and agrees to abide by all interplanetary regulations. This authorizes the cadet to participate in all club activities."

Bamberg/Zoomar sometimes figured into Normandale presentations and promotions that involved Channel 20.

"'Captain Zoomar' used to give away prizes and play movies for the kids from a kiosk in the center of the Normandale parking lot while their parents shopped," recalled Bamberg's son David. "Many of the Normandale merchants advertised on WCOV-TV programs, including the Captain Zoomar show."

Bamberg/Zoomar would appear at individual stores in Normandale,

MEET
CAPTAIN ZOOMAR
IN PERSON AT
SAULS
Monday Evening
6 P.M. 'Til 9 P.M.

CAPTAIN ZOOMAR
Will Have A Treasure Bag
For All Boys and Girls

as well as at locations such as the Paramount Theatre downtown.

The elder Bamberg also did standard news reporting and interviews for Channel 20.

The Normandale merchants also worked with WSFA-TV (Channel 12, an NBC affiliate), which went on the air in late 1954.

THE NINTH ANNIVERSARY IN 1963 seemed to be slightly subdued, as the merchants concentrated on their own ads.

Nevertheless, the theme of the anniversary was announced as "An Entire World of Fashions for Living." A week-long celebration presented numerous performances and events under the aegis of new Normandale Merchants' Association president Dave Bronson and Meredith Harrell.

Of primary interest to shoppers was a contest to win an all-expenses-paid trip for two to Nassau, Bahamas via Delta Airlines. The winner was Mildred McLean of Montgomery, an employee of the State Revenue Department. She and her husband Claude had never been out

*Walter Bamberg interviews Paul Brinegar and Clint Eastwood, who portrayed Wishbone and Rowdy Yates, respectively, on the legendary CBS Western* Rawhide— *courtesy of David Bamberg.*

*From left, Jack Sweigart, Meredith Harrell, Mildred McLean, Claude McLean.*

of the United States. They were presented with their tickets by Delta Airlines representative Jack Sweigart and Harrell.

Entertainment during the anniversary was provided by Joe Phillips and his trained animals. The Sidney Lanier High School drill team also performed, as did the Robert E. Lee High School band. Other innovations included live models in store windows and a "strolling orchestra."

IN THE EARLY 1960S, the football rivalry between

Lee and Lanier was full-throttle. Some years the annual end-of-the-season football game between the two Montgomery schools would fill Cramton Bowl, while the annual Blue-Gray college all-star game wouldn't sell out.

Woolworth's stores in Normandale and Eastbrook gave away free pompoms, blue-and-white to Lanier High fans and red-and-white to Lee High supporters. Carver High was not mentioned.

BEAUTY QUEENS WERE ALSO still popular in the Capital City. Montgomery's Dinah Washington, who represented Alabama at that year's Miss Universe contest, was honored at the Lee band concert at Normandale.

In a published update for the anniversary, Dave Bronson also welcomed Al Levy's, a branch of the downtown Montgomery women's fashion store.

In mid-September of 1963, the Dallas-based Zale's Jewelers chain, acquired Norman Jewelers in the Normandale arcade. The transition included using both names ("Zale's-Norman Jewelers") for a limited time. Esther and Joe Fleischman continued to work at the store.

AS WITH ANY SHOPPING center, some stores eventually departed from Normandale and other businesses moved into the available spaces. In addition to Al Levy's, Fannin's (men's clothing) and Dexter Interiors (fine furniture and decorating) were downtown retailers, so the opening of branch stores in Normandale added to the shopping center's prestige and viability.

Dexter Interiors—sometimes advertised as

*Joe Fleischman proffers a bracelet to a customer following the acquisition of Norman Jewelers by Zale's Jewelers—PR.*

business. Lisa recalled that her mother decorated the Governor's Mansion, the State Capitol, and the George Wallaces' home when they moved out of the Governor's Mansion. She later did decorating in Tuskegee for members of the nationally popular Commodores singing group.

The younger Segall had a wistful attitude about being in a family that ran a successful business in Normandale. "My twin sister and I helped out in both the downtown store and in Normandale during the summer and on holidays from school," Lisa recounted. "In fact, we were models in the windows for the Christmas display. It was really a great open-air mall. We could walk there from our home to shop and to see our parents and hit them up for lunch money. We'd often meet our friends there . . . several of our parent's friends also owned stores there and I remember that when we were there, we always stopped by to say hello to the parents of our friends. It was really a great community."

"Dexters Interiors"—opened on September 30, 1963, in the former Roslyn Eagle store in the arcade. "Dexter Interiors carried brands such as Henredon, Century, Drexel-Heritage, Sherrill, and Thomasville, to name a few," recalled Lisa Segall, whose parents, Sara and Sigmund Segall, owned the stores with Sari and Sam Chernau, Mr. Segall's sister and brother-in-law. "In addition to furniture and a 'fine' gift shop, they had fabric, and a workroom for both upholstery and draperies. They were, at that time, the only fine furniture store in Alabama."

Dexter Interiors would later open a separate store in Normandale for their drapery and upholstery

THE ONGOING CIVIL RIGHTS movement meant that many white Alabamians, including numerous state politicians, weren't fans of the country's new, young president. John F. Kennedy was an advocate for civil rights and was developing legislation to ban segregation.

The afternoon of November 22, 1963, would be memorable for all Americans, including some who were at Normandale that day. Pike Road's George Howell was an eleventh grader at Sidney Lanier High School. "In early November 1963," he recalled, "the Christian Youth Fellowship— C. Y. F.—of the First Christian Church decided to have a bake sale on the sidewalk at Loveman's on the afternoon of Friday, November 22nd. We had cookies and slices of cake wrapped up in plastic wrap but I don't remember why we needed to raise money. After we got word that President Kennedy had been killed in Dallas that afternoon, we thought about postponing the sale, but then we decided to go ahead anyway. In those days, the public in Montgomery did not seem too bothered about losing Kennedy.

"My cousin Mary Moores was in the twelfth grade. After school, Mary drove us out to Normandale. Somebody else was running the sale, and we gave them the cake my mother had made. I remembered that Loveman's sold television sets upstairs, behind the big window where they had Santa Claus every year. I went up the escalator—which was always a treat—and found the TV sets. One was turned on with the volume up. I saw Lyndon Johnson take the oath of office on the airplane, with Jackie Kennedy standing next to him in her pink, blood-stained suit. When they were ready to leave Dallas, I went back down to the bake sale.

"The people passing by on the sidewalk seemed somewhat subdued that afternoon, and I think we didn't make much money from the sale. But we carried on until dark—about 5:30. When we were closing down the sale, I went back up into Loveman's and watched Air Force One on the ramp at Andrews Air Force Base. I saw them unload the coffin through a side door in the back. Military guards put the coffin in a hearse, and it drove away. Back downstairs, my cousins and I left Normandale to drive home to Pike Road. It was an odd afternoon for me, but I remember it well."

A UNIQUE PROMOTION WAS set up in the rear of the arcade for several days in early December 1963. Space flight was in its infancy, and Earthlings were fascinated by the primeval voyages into the void

by American astronauts and Soviet cosmonauts. Locally, the Sputnik Drive-In, named after the first satellite to orbit the Earth, had opened out on the Mobile Highway, and an outer space/science fiction movie was often the feature film at the Saturday morning "Kiddie Matinee" (admission was fifteen cents) at the Clover Theatre on Fairview Avenue.

The U.S.-U.S.S.R. competition begat the term "Space Race," and the Moon was the ultimate prize.

To exploit this new phenomenon, a portable, 72-foot-long "rocket ship" ride was temporarily installed in the Normandale arcade between Al Levy's and the A&P grocery. The ride had originally been an early tourist attraction in Gatlinburg, Tennessee, gateway to the Great Smoky Mountains. The vehicle was named the 'Smoky Comet," and it was transported to shopping centers and other locations in numerous states as a transient, modernistic carnival ride of sorts.

"Passengers" were seated in the interior, which was eight feet in diameter. Hydraulic movement of the "spacecraft" was enhanced with video and other primeval special effects. Curiously, the ad for the attraction included a drawing of passengers inside, and almost all were wearing hats, as if fashionably dressed for a (simulated) journey into space.

DURING THE 1960s, MANY junior high boys—most of whom went to nearby Floyd Junior High

School—often rode their bikes to Normandale just to "hang out" (i.e., loiter), and a favorite gathering spot was in the rear of the arcade between Woolworth's and Grant's, near the entrance to the community center/fallout shelter. Some kids had paper routes, and that location was also a drop-off point where boys would pick up their respective bundles of newspapers to deliver to homes.

Schwinn Sting-Ray bicycles (or similar models) were a fad at the time. Introduced in 1963, Sting-Rays had gawky-looking "ape hanger" handlebars and elongated "banana" seats. Many base models didn't have fenders over the tires, which could be disastrous to the rider on a wet street.

Such a cosmetically odd bicycle could be purchased right there in Normandale. Western Auto was among the retailers who sold clones of the Sting-Ray; their Western Flyer-branded copy was known as the Buzz Bike. Unsurprisingly, "Sting-Ray" became the generic name for bicycles of that style. Of course, Western Auto sold "standard" configurations of bicycles for boys and girls as well.

Ultimately, some boys were able to acquire cheap motorcycles such as the popular Honda 50, which made for faster daily coverage of a paper route.

OCCASIONALLY, BOREDOM COMPELLED SOME kids (who presumably didn't deliver papers) to head out from the rear of the arcade to a pre-selected store to commit some (usually harmless) prank. One popular act of sabotage was jamming the Loveman's elevators to prevent them from aligning with the floor when they reached the ground level.

"A buddy and I used to jump up and down right before the elevator would come to its resting place," one rogue recalled, "and it would stop about a foot above the floor. The Loveman's employees finally caught us and told us to leave."

Many of the pimple-faced diversionists went about their furtive mischief in abject terror of the store detective at Loveman's.

"Once, (a friend) and I turned the nozzle of the electric hand dryer in the men's restroom at Loveman's upside down and filled it with water," recalled another would-be saboteur. "The idea was that the next visitor wouldn't notice and would get a face full of water when he turned it on. Luckily, we weren't electrocuted, along with a potential victim. Somehow, we got caught by that tall, gray-haired lady detective."

Loveman's store detective Ellen Graves was indeed a large-framed female with a voguish silver coiffure. She was an early female employee in what was stereotypically a man's career field. She was often seen in a dapper solid color blazer and matching or coordinating solid-color skirt. When necessary, her serious countenance was intimidating to most adolescent boys.

"If I knew she was around, I wouldn't do nothin'," one Baby Boomer admitted.

"She had a great personality, but she could be tough," Dick McAdams said appreciatively.

Other Normandale employees also made lasting impressions on youngsters. One individual recalled "the gruff owner-cashier with thick glasses at Joy's restaurant."

*The Full House, a typical Montgomery teenage rock band of the era. From left, Tom Brantley, Mike Mardis, Tommy Widener, Steve Evans—courtesy of Tom Brantley.*

THROUGHOUT THE 1960S, MANY local musical groups performed at Normandale. The location of the performances varied based on the projected size of the audience. The parking lot was still viable, but combos with more equipment might end up on a flatbed trailer if the usual portable stage was too small. Sometimes the stage or trailer was stationed at the entrance to the breezeway. Some bands performed *inside* the breezeway, albeit not on an elevated stage.

The interest in playing in a rock band abruptly increased for teenage males following the Beatles' appearance on *The Ed Sullivan Show* in early 1964—here was a way to meet girls besides being a jock! You could play in a band! The number of teen combos that sprang up across the country was unfathomable. Such aggregations would ultimately be nicknamed "garage bands"—because that's where many of them rehearsed.

Accordingly, performances by such combos at

Normandale would add a boost to their credibility.

THE TENTH ANNIVERSARY OF Normandale in 1964 seemed to be relatively low-key, perhaps because of a collective perspective that Normandale had settling into retail dominance in central Alabama. Some merchants cited the birthday in their respective ads, and Meredith Harrell still developed and staged promotional events.

Unique occurrences were ongoing—free pancakes were dispensed in the arcade on October 1, courtesy of Aunt Jemima pancake mix and the Normandale Merchants' Association.

A disproportionate number of merchants were Jewish, and many lived with their families in the

Normandale subdivision. Accordingly, the number of Jewish students at Floyd Junior High School was noticeably higher than at other junior highs in Montgomery. Immature slurs such as "Jerusalem Junior High" were sometimes heard from white kids from elsewhere.

Adolescent bigotry aside, a list of holiday store closings was published each fall before many Jewish-owned businesses shut down for Yom Kippur. The adjacent 1965 list included eleven stores in Normandale.

Normandale's two "giant Easter Bunnies," Norman and Dale, continued to patrol the premises each spring. They participated in awards presentations for some promotions that were oriented towards youngsters, such as coloring contests.

WHEN THE ELEVENTH BIRTHDAY of Normandale rolled around in 1965, advertisements perked up as the Normandale Merchants' Association gave away

## IN OBSERVANCE OF
# RELIGIOUS HOLIDAY
## THE FOLLOWING STORES
# WILL BE CLOSED
# ALL DAY TOMORROW
## Wednesday, October 6

| | |
|---|---|
| **Alex Rice**<br>DOWNTOWN | **Montgomery Shoe Factory**<br>3 LOCATIONS<br>NORMANDALE—DOWNTOWN—EASTBROOK |
| **A. Nachman's**<br>Bennington—Owners<br>DOWNTOWN AND IN NORMANDALE | |
| **Berns Jewelers**<br>DOWNTOWN | **The Record Shop**<br>NORMANDALE ARCADE |
| **Bronson's**<br>ON THE MALL<br>NORMANDALE | **City Pawn Shop**<br>9 N. COURT STREET |
| **Dexter Interiors**<br>DOWNTOWN AND IN NORMANDALE | **Shinbaum's**<br>THE COMPLETE STORE FOR MEN<br>39 S. COURT & GUNTER AFB<br>CLOSES 4 P.M. TUESDAY |
| **Four Seasons**<br>CLOVERLAND SHOPPING CENTER | |
| **Lou Herman's**<br>NORMANDALE | **Teens 'n' Tweens**<br>NORMANDALE |
| **The Hub**<br>DOWNTOWN | **Toyland**<br>NORMANDALE |
| **Jay's**<br>DOWNTOWN | **The Village Store**<br>NORMANDALE |
| **Al Levy's**<br>DOWNTOWN AND IN NORMANDALE | **Weils'**<br>DOWNTOWN |
| **Montgomery Rug & Shade Co., Inc.**<br>DOWNTOWN | **Yardstick, Inc.**<br>NORMANDALE |

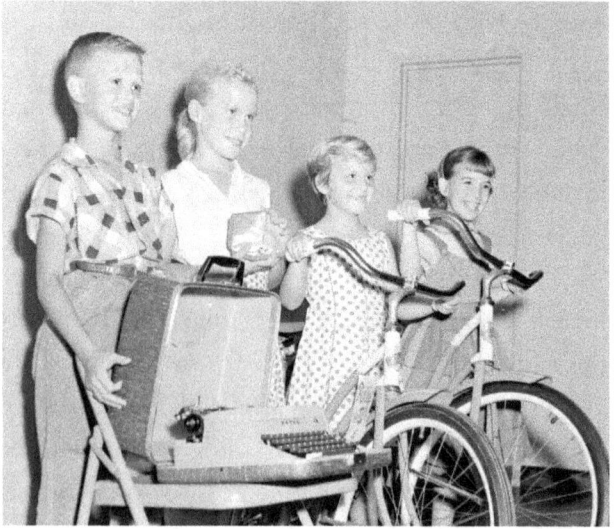

*Top, Norman and Dale with a coloring contest winner. Bottom, these four kids won two bicycles, a watch, and a typewriter—PR.*

six color televisions. All in all, the retail outlook for Normandale Shopping City for the second half of the decade was promising.

In late September, Meredith Harrell appeared in a quasi-endorsement ad for the *Montgomery Advertiser* and *Alabama Journal* combined-issue sports pages.

MORE THAN ONE NEARBY business exploited its proximity to the Normandale Shopping City. Shakey's Pizza, a national chain that had been founded California in 1954, had rapidly expanded across the country, offering pizza served in an "old-timey" atmosphere with appropriate live music (one wonders how many banjo players "gigged" at Shakey's).

The Shakey's restaurant in Montgomery was located behind Normandale on Winston Drive, just across from the shopping center's rear parking

*Left, Meredith Harrell publicity photo. Below, Ann Holland poses in front of the arcade fountain, which, while shut down during the winter months, was still decorated for the Christmas season.—courtesy of Ann McMeans.*

lot behind W. T. Grant's. It stayed busy as a popular gathering place for customers of all ages.

Normandale continued to elaborately decorate its premises for the Christmas shopping season, and Santa Claus performed his duties annually in the right-facing upstairs display window at Loveman's. His appearance at that location in Normandale was now a tradition, eagerly expected by children and their parents.

"I have such happy childhood memories of Normandale,' said Nancy Evans, "particularly visiting the *real* Santa sitting in the large window inside Loveman's. Year after year at Christmastime, as you pulled into the big Normandale parking lot, all you had to do was look up and you saw him in that second-story window, with a line of children ready to sit in his lap and tell him what they wanted for Christmas. Knowing that I would be up there in that window in just a few minutes doing the same was beyond magical."

*Below left, Derilyn Lavender with Santa, ca. 1962—courtesy of Derilyn Lee; below right, Nancy Evans with Santa, 1964—courtesy of Nancy Evans.*

# 11

# Cruise Control

As Normandale continued its retail dominance in central and south Alabama during the latter half of the 1960s, Meredith Harrell kept the shopping center's unique promotions ongoing at a steady pace. Some were so well-received that they were brought back "by popular demand." For example, more than one cookout competition was held in the mid-to-late 1960s.

Other promotions included fashion shows, Jett's Petting Zoo, and Skipper the Performing Porpoise.

Dick McAdams's hole-in-the-wall carpet company in Normandale continued to prosper and win awards. In 1966, McAdams Carpets received two first-place awards, one from a Georgia-Alabama organization and one from the Montgomery Advertising Club for best use of newspaper color advertising.

One Sidewalk Sale in July 1966 had a whimsical/humorous facet, as members of the Normandale Merchants' Association dressed in spiffy striped vests and bowler hats for an advertisement (photo, next page).

Leo Chrietzberg parted ways with Parker-Sledge Hardware in 1966 and moved to Wetumpka as a partner with his Uncle Hap at M. H. Harden Hardware.

"Even though Hap was his uncle, they were very close in age," said Barry Chrietzburg, "and Hap was, to me, much closer than a great-uncle. Hap had been trying to lure my dad into the business with him for some time."

In early October 1966, Aaron Aronov was the keynote speaker at the International Council of Shopping Centers' Annual Promotion Conference in Washington, D.C. Meredith Harrell was

**Normandale Shopping City**

PRESENTS

**JETT'S PETTING ZOO**

Appearing
Thru
March 20th

**Admission**

with special merchants
discount ticket . . . . 15¢

without ticket . . . . . 25¢

*Attraction Open During
Shopping Center Hours*

Pick up discount tickets
*from*
Any Normandale Store

Tame Baby and Midget Animals

**NORMANDALE SHOPPING CITY**

an active member of that organization and also attended the conference.

IN JANUARY 1967, HARRELL was profiled in the local newspaper's "Montgomery Laymen" series as someone ". . . whose active church work contributes toward making our community a better place to live." The article cited Harrell, a member of Dalraida Methodist Church, for his multi-faceted work with his church, the Heart Fund, and the Boy Scouts, as well as his membership in the Kiwanis Club and the International Council of Shopping Centers.

In the spring of the same year, a fast food restaurant chain called Burger Ranch opened its fourth Montgomery location in Normandale. There was also a Pizza Presto in the shopping center in those

*Normandale Merchants' Association members dress up for a 1966 promotion: from left, front: Bernie Gross, Raymond Cohen, Don Blevins; back: Meredith Harrell, Lou Herman, Leo Chrietzberg, Walter Klemurray.*

times. The shopping center combined its thirteenth anniversary and "Back to School Days" sale in late August.

Eastbrook was still a factor in the competition between local shopping centers. Popular eastside would-be griot Charles Casmus, an aspiring drummer as a teenager, recalled that he had bought his first record album at W. T. Grant in Eastbrook. However, Casmus later came across town to Normandale in search of LPs, because of the larger selection. Like Eastbrook, Normandale also had W. T. Grant and F. W. Woolworth stores, both of which stocked albums. But the Record Shop was living up to its name, and Loveman's also had a record department.

"Obviously, I wish there'd been a Record Shop in Eastbrook!" Casmus said. "They had started with selling just albums and 45s. Later, they got into stereos and eight-track tapes."

THE SPRINGTIME APPEARANCE OF "Norman and Dale" was an annual tradition at Normandale, and Jane Laseter was in high school in 1969 when she was hired to be a giant Easter Bunny.

"It was my first-ever job," she recalled. "The outfit was three pieces—head, body, and feet. I walked around handing out Easter eggs and candy to children. I remember the outfit was *hot*. I would go into Liger's Bakery to remove the head and breathe in some air-conditioned air."

Lee's Drugs moved out of their store in Normandale in 1969 and was replaced by Normandale Drugs, a new business owned by local pharmacists Barry Blondheim and Alan Rosenthal.

At the end of the decade, Dick McAdams moved his carpet business into a large new building on the Eastern By-Pass.

"Everything was going good at Normandale, but I wanted to be able to carry rolled goods in my store," the company founder explained. "The new building was about 20,000 square feet, and I was out there early. Nix-Godwin (Furniture) was next to me."

*September, 1969: New officers for the Normandale Merchants' Association included, clockwise from left: Bennie Witt (Toyland), treasurer; Arnold Unger (Loveman's), vice-president, and Walter Brenner (Montgomery Shoe Factory), president.*

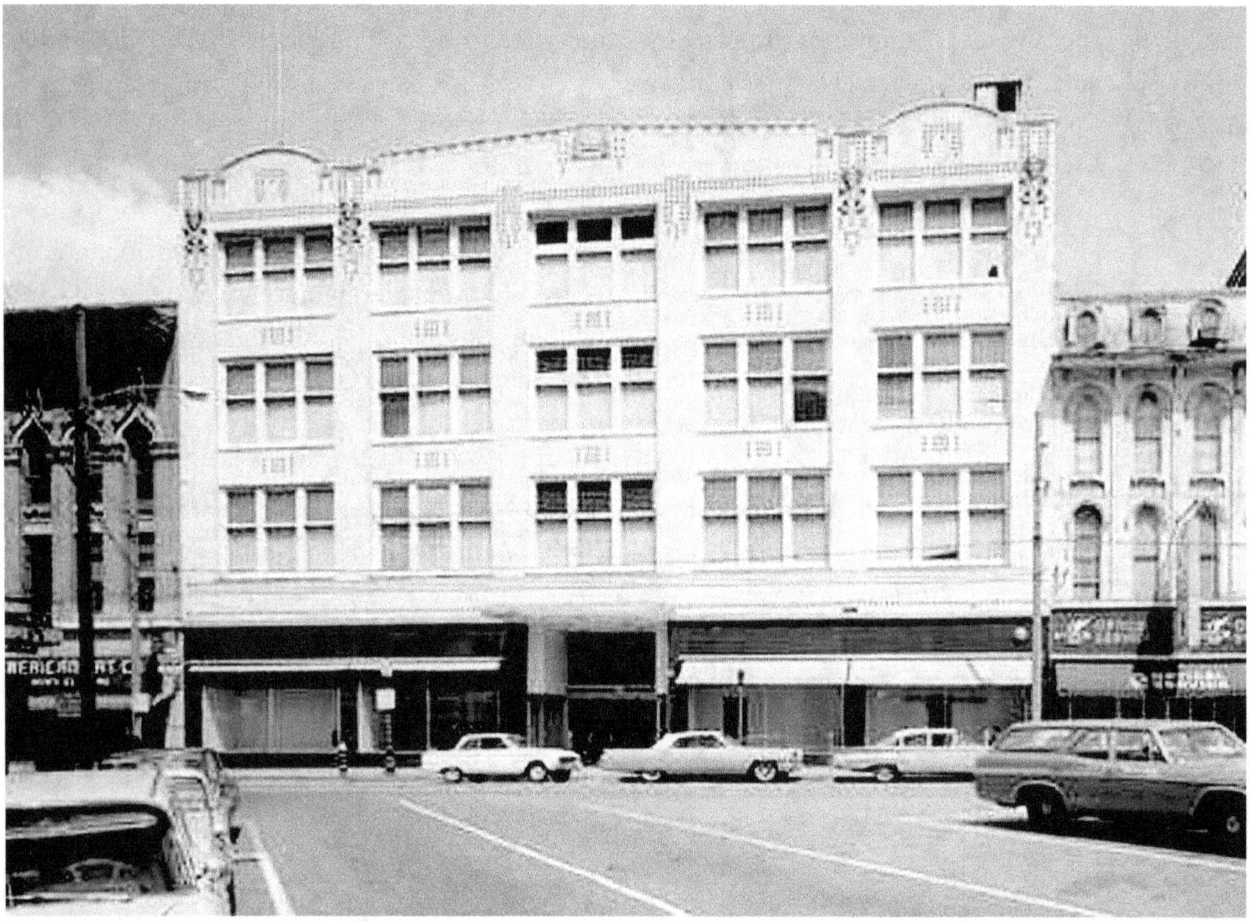

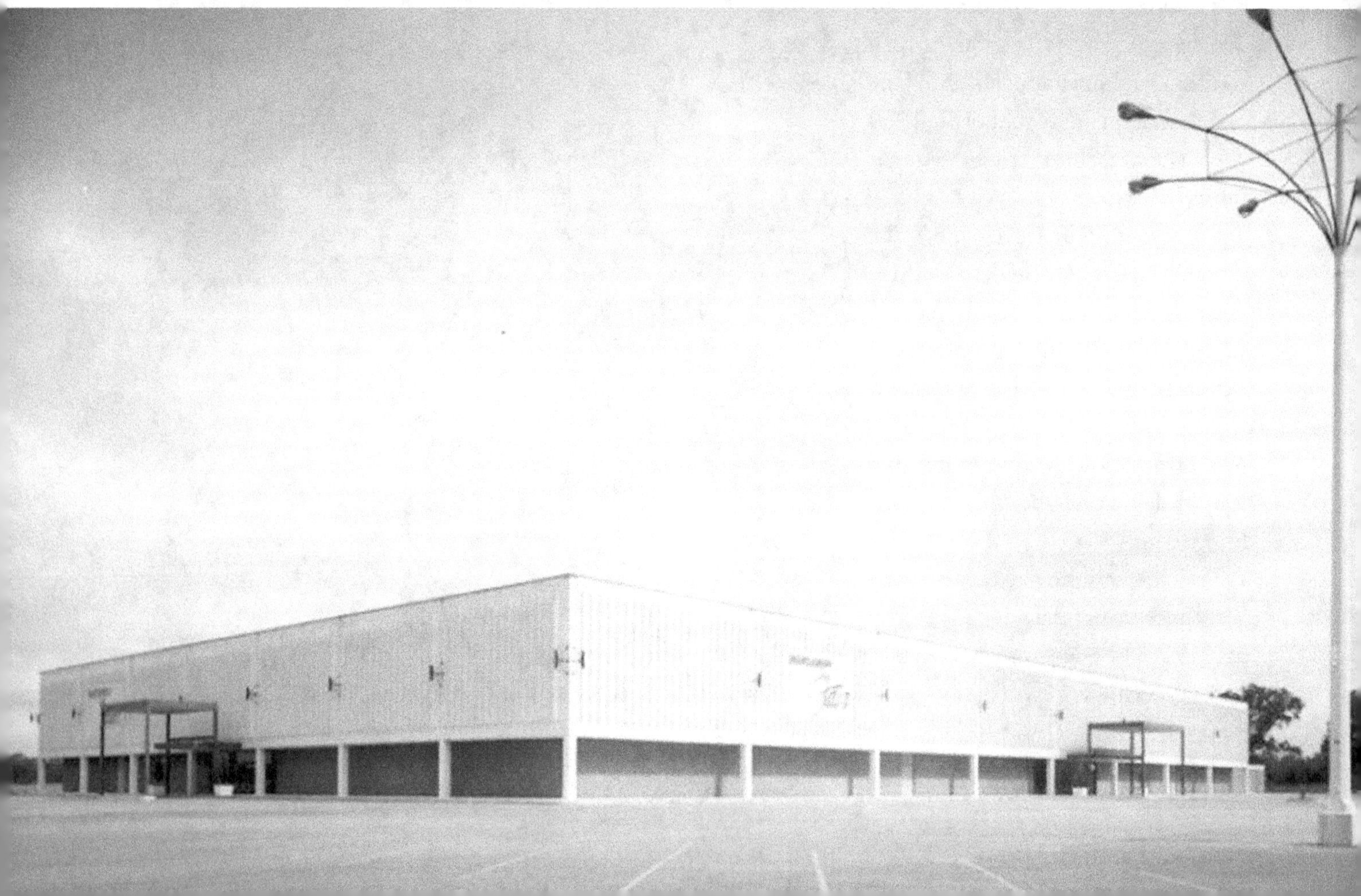

# 12

# Seismic Shifts to the East

Many older Montgomery residents will point to the 1970 establishment of Montgomery Mall in southeast Montgomery as an initial omen regarding the future of Normandale. However, one of Montgomery Mall's original anchor stores had relocated from downtown Montgomery several years earlier.

In the mid-twentieth century, Montgomery Fair department stores were located in Florence, Greenville, Andalusia, Anniston, Tuskegee, Tallassee and Opelika.

Montgomery Fair's flagship and headquarters store had been the largest department store in downtown Montgomery, with merchandise on three floors and a mezzanine. Rosa Parks was working as a seamstress for that store when she was arrested on December 1, 1955. She was subsequently fired from Montgomery Fair.

Another employee, Mildred Henley, started out as an elevator operator in the downtown store, and remained with the Capital City retailer for forty-eight years, retiring as office manager some years after the move to southeast Montgomery.

*Facing page, top: Montgomery Fair's store on Dexter Avenue in downtown Montgomery; bottom, the Fair's new location at what would become Montgomery Mall. —ADAH.*

By the 1970s, the Fair had three stores remaining, including the massive stand-alone new store in southeast Montgomery, which opened on February 18, 1965, at the three-thoroughfare intersection of the Southern By-Pass, the Eastern By-Pass and McGehee Road. Alabama Governor George Wallace had cut the ribbon at the grand opening ceremony.

The Montgomery Fair stores in Eastbrook Shopping Center and Opelika were also still viable. The downtown store closed after the new southeast two-story free-standing store was completed.

The Montgomery Fair group was a member of a national consortium of department stores called Mercantile Stores Company, Inc. The Gayfer's department store chain, headquartered in Mobile, was also affiliated with Mercantile Stores.

After Montgomery Fair's move from downtown, efforts began to consolidate the two brands to facilitate a branded credit card's use at a Montgomery group store or a Mobile group store. The three Montgomery Fair stores went by "Gayfer's/Montgomery Fair" for a period of transition, after which only "Gayfer's" was used.

Montgomery Mall was then created when national retailer J. C. Penney built a store opposite Gayfer's/Montgomery Fair, and a line-up of stereotypical "mall shops"—Orange Julius, Singer Sewing Center, National Shirt Shops, etc.—connected the two anchor units to create Montgomery's first indoor shopping mall. The most prominent eatery was Morrison's Cafeteria.

A later expansion opened in 1988, anchored by Parisian, a department store chain headquartered in Birmingham.

OBVIOUSLY, MEREDITH HARRELL AND the Normandale merchants were paying close attention to the business activities of Montgomery Mall, and most Normandale retailers were also aware of research that indicated the city was continuing to move in an eastward direction.

Normandale promotions continued unabated, as exemplified by the back-by-popular-demand Jett's Petting Zoo and annual Sidewalk Sales

1971

(sometimes more than one in the same year). Perhaps the legacy of Zippy the Chimp was influential, since one of the 1971 Normandale promotions was an appearance by the Lipko Comedy Chimps.

Some ads began to promote the longevity of Normandale Shopping Center ("Montgomery's Oldest"). In 1973–74, a series of ads had a succinct phrase, "Off the Beaten By-Pass—Norman Bridge at Patton," situated in a corner of the layout.

THE 1970s SAW THE massive retail mecca undergoing profound changes.

Bronson's changed its name to "The Name

**NOW THRU SAT.**

**NORMANDALE**
Consistent With Our Policy of Bringing The Very Finest to Normandale Shoppers . . . Whether It Be In Merchandise or "Added Attractions" . . . We're Happy To Present A

**ON THE ARCADE IN NORMANDALE NOW THRU SATURDAY**

**HILL COUNTRY**

**CRAFT SHOW**
★ MUSIC ★ ART ★ CRAFTS
A GRAND ASSEMBLY OF MEN AND WOMEN ACTUALLY AT WORK AT THE AGE-OLD OCCUPATIONS THAT HAVE MADE THE MOUNTAIN COUNTRY AMERICA'S MOST POPULAR TOURIST AREA. NOW FOR THREE DAYS, THEY'VE MOVED LOCK, STOCK AND BARREL TO

**THE ARCADE..IN NORMANDALE**

*1971*

**NORMANDALE'S BIG**
**Oktober**
**SIDEWALK SALE**
ALL DAY SATURDAY
ONE BIG DAY (SATURDAY) ON THE SIDEWALKS OF N'DALE!

*1977*

**JUST 4 HOURS**
**SUNDOWN SALE**
**TONIGHT 5 TIL 9**
IN THE SHOPPING CENTER "WHERE IT'S HAPPENING"
**NORMANDALE**

*1977*

**NORMANDALE'S**
GIGANTIC ONCE-A-YEAR
**Fall SIDEWALK Festival**
WHOPPING BARGAINS ALL OVER NORMANDALE!
ONE BIG DAY OF SUPER-VALUES!
ALL DAY SATURDAY OCT. 25

*1975*

**Normandale's**
**SIDEWALK Savings**
**EVENT**
Colossal Bargains on the Sidewalk
Live Entertainment by JACK TURNER'S Blue Grass Band
JUST ONE BIG SALE DAY!!!
SATURDAY, JUNE 17th
ALL YOUR FAVORITE STORES PLUS • NEW BARRY'S TRAVEL CENTER
• NEW HANCOCK FABRICS • SOUND SHOP • LIGER'S BAKERY
• ENLARGED MONTGOMERY SHOE & LUGGAGE • KNIT 'N STITCH

*1977*

**PRE JULY 4th Sidewalk Sale NORMANDALE**
SATURDAY
C'MON!! JOIN US
SAT..!! 10:00 A.M. 'TIL 5:45 P.M.

*1976*

Make plans now to attend the
**MONTGOMERY ART GUILD SHOW**
Saturday, May 12
You'll be sure to find something special for Mom or for yourself. Don't miss it!
**Normandale**

*1979*

YOU'RE INVITED TO ATTEND THE
MONTGOMERY FEDERATION OF GARDEN CLUB'S
**COUNTRY FAIR**
SATURDAY . . . MARCH 19
9:30 A.M. TIL 4:00 P.M.
ON SALE!!
THOUSANDS OF HAND MADE ITEMS
MADE BY MEMBERS OF THE GARDEN CLUBS
ON THE ARCADE — IN
**NORMANDALE**

*1977*

**NORMANDALE SHOPPING CENTER**
"MONTGOMERY'S OLDEST"
**YOUR VALUE STOP**
ALL DAY SATURDAY
• FASHIONS
• SHOES
• FURNITURE
• TOYS
Something For All Ages At Low, Low Prices!

*1978*

**SIDEWALK Normandale's Sale!**
All day Saturday June 9 Don't you miss it!

*1979*

**ALL DAY SATURDAY Normandale ANNUAL HARVEST SIDEWALK SALE**
Sat., Oct. 20th, 10 til 6  Time Again To Reap The Best Bargains!

*1979*

**STREET FAIR SIDEWALK SALE**
**SATURDAY ON THE SIDEWALKS OF Normandale**
JUST ONE BIG DAY... ALL DAY SAT.
COLOSSAL BARGAINS ON THE SIDEWALK! ENTERTAINMENT BY THE RHYTHMACES

*1977*

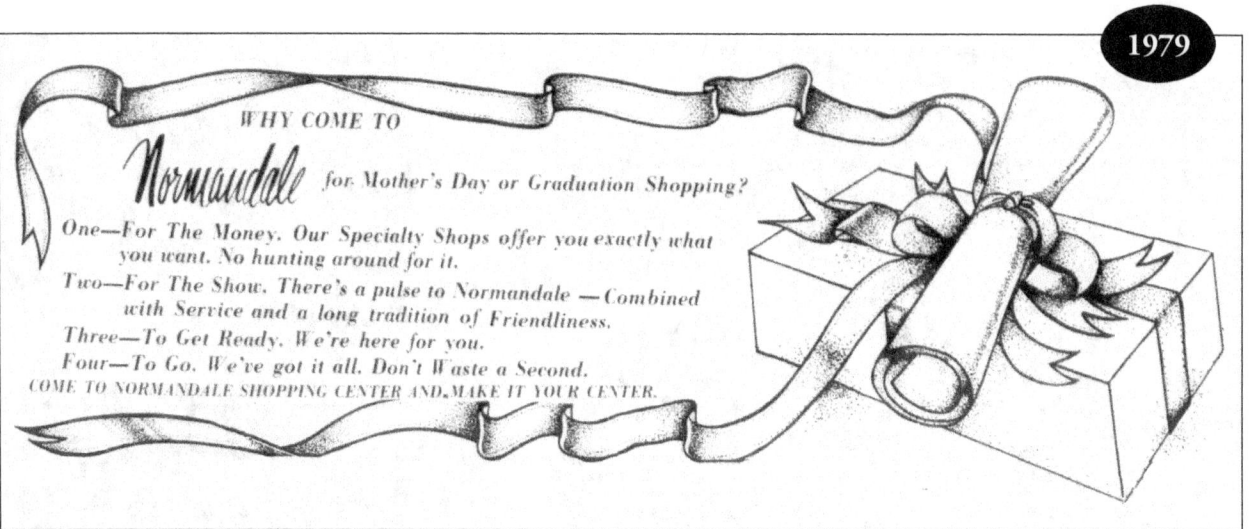

1979

WHY COME TO

*Normandale* for Mother's Day or Graduation Shopping?

One—For The Money. Our Specialty Shops offer you exactly what you want. No hunting around for it.

Two—For The Show. There's a pulse to Normandale—Combined with Service and a long tradition of Friendliness.

Three—To Get Ready. We're here for you.

Four—To Go. We've got it all. Don't Waste a Second.

COME TO NORMANDALE SHOPPING CENTER AND MAKE IT YOUR CENTER.

Dropper" in 1971. DeShields-Larson Shoes had been sold to the Brown Shoe Company, a national firm, in 1968, but the new owners retained the familiar name and continued to operate the Normandale store. Dave Larson remained with the stores until 1973. The Francis Cafeteria closed in 1972, and its lower-level space was taken over by Culp Piano & Organ Company.

Yancey Liger had died in 1965 but his widow, Florence, continued to run the family's business. She eventually sold Liger's Bakery, and the new owners moved it to a strip mall called Gay Meadows Shopping Center, located down McGehee Road about two miles from Montgomery Mall. "The cost of running a private bakery that used all real ingredients made competing with the [grocery store] chains difficult," grandson Tony Radford commented. "Granny was never willing to change any of our legacy recipes."

A WOULD-BE-HIP STORE CALLED Pant-A-Rama opened in August 1972 in the front line space formerly occupied by Parker-Sledge Hardware. The new retailer specialized in blue jeans. A local rock band called the Ozella Flesh Band played for the grand opening of Pant-A-Rama. Drummer Charles Casmus recalled that his combo performed in front of the store instead of the entrance to the arcade breezeway, where most live musical performances were presented.

Pant-A-Rama had a unique advertising gimmick—the store's cartoon mascot was a super-hero, Captain Britches, who was shown in his own three-panel presentation on the comics pages of the local newspapers, right next to Broom-Hilda, Steve

*Charles Casmus and guitarist John Bedsole of the Ozella Flesh Band perform for Pant-A-Rama's grand opening—courtesy of Charles Casmus.*

1973

Canyon, and other characters. Such an innovation looked like it was right in place, but close inspection revealed a designation for "advertisement" next to the Captain Britches strip.

BY 1973, FLACK'S HAD begun inserting a somewhat-assertive tag line in its print ads that read "A store of women, for women, run by a woman" (the singular female being Bernice Basch).

The next year, a change in the ownership of Flack's was announced. Several former Belk's department store management officials had left that company and were acquiring smaller clothing stores to form a regional chain called "Mr. A's Ltd.," named after longtime Belk's honcho Richard "Dick" Avery, who had managed the Montgomery Belk-Hudson store on Dexter Avenue for a number of years and was now the head of the new company.

Such acquisitions by Avery and associates included Flack's in Normandale. The store's name

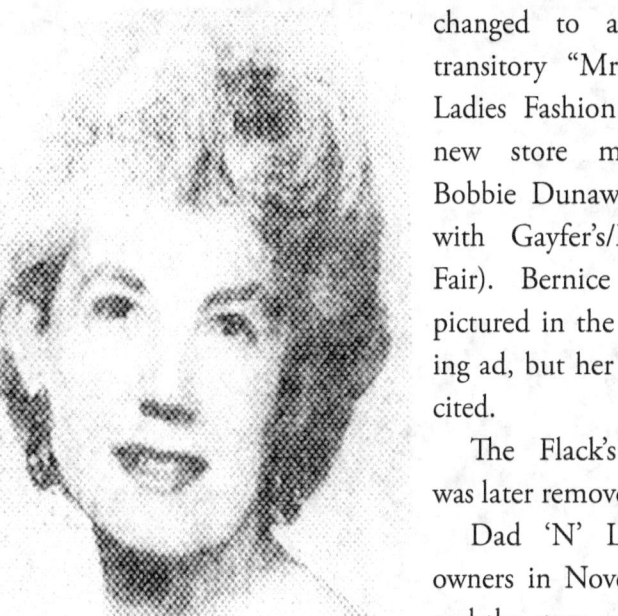

*Bernice Basch, 1974.*

changed to an obviously transitory "Mr. A's Flack's Ladies Fashion Shop." The new store manager was Bobbie Dunaway (formerly with Gayfer's/Montgomery Fair). Bernice Basch was pictured in the grand opening ad, but her title was not cited.

The Flack's appellation was later removed.

Dad 'N' Lad changed owners in November 1973, and the store name changed to Richards—Clothes for the Lionhearted. A "Formerly Dad 'N Lad" tag would be seen in advertising for a brief time.

BORN IN THE MID-1970S, Montgomery writer Foster Dickson grew up in the Normandale subdivision. He recalled appearances by Santa Claus at Loveman's throughout his childhood. On at least one occasion, St. Nick rode into the Normandale parking lot accompanied by a group of Shriners

I'd ride my bike around. The police at Normandale would fuss at us if they caught us riding our bikes on the sidewalk."

In April 1974, Meredith Harrell was the subject of a *Montgomery Advertiser* "Retail Profile." That ongoing series featured local business leaders accompanied by line drawing portraits by Tom Connor.

Faye Foster (Dickson) Singleton

The article referred to Harrell as the "promotions director" for Normandale Shopping Center, and noted that he had the same responsibility for other Aronov shopping centers in Alabama, Mississippi, and Tennessee. His membership in the International Council of Shopping Centers was also cited.

During the nation's Bicentennial year, 1976, the deadly H1N1 influenza strain, better known as "swine flu," came rampaging out of Fort Dix, New Jersey. The federal government responded with a nationwide immunization program, setting up ad hoc stations at popular public locations. Normandale and other shopping centers were among the Montgomery locations for temporary single-function medical facilities.

and Ronald McDonald in a jalopy fire engine. Dickson also remembered a statue of Santa seated on a throne being displayed near the intersection of Patton Avenue and Norman Bridge Road.

"Everything we did was there," he said. "We rode our bicycles to Normandale almost every day. We shopped for groceries at Winn-Dixie, and the Heart Association had offices above Culp Piano. My mother's aunt worked there, so my mom was a volunteer. I would go with her and help out, or

Dexter Interiors's second store in Normandale opened in mid-1976, in the arcade space formerly occupied by Al Levy's. The new store was known as Dexter Interiors' Fabric Center, as it handled the company's upholstery and drapery business. The other store was advertised as the "Furniture Center."

The W. T. Grant national chain filed for

bankruptcy in 1976. When its Normandale store was vacated, the space it had occupied at the end of the arcade became a Hancock Fabrics store.

A "SECOND-VERSE-SAME-AS-THE-FIRST" DIEGESIS HAPPENED in 1977, when Eastdale Mall, Montgomery's second fully enclosed shopping center, opened at the intersection of the Eastern By-Pass and the Atlanta Highway. In its ultimate configuration, it would have *four* anchor units and an indoor ice skating rink. And it was an Aronov project.

Raymond Cohen was friends with the owners of Cobb-Kirkland Motor Co. and Montgomery Rug and Shade, whose businesses were located on the Eastern By-Pass. They began encouraging him to relocate eastward, as the city was growing in that direction. Investing in the ownership of a building instead paying monthly rent was also an attraction.

After twenty years at Normandale, the Record Shop moved to the Eastern By-Pass in 1977. The new location's main building had a 15,000-square foot sales floor with a 6,400-square foot warehouse.

*Left, Normandale "Patio Sale" promotions in the mid-1970s were aimed at females and offered average folks a chance to run their own patio sales (forerunner of yard sales) at no charge. Above, promotion for the shopping center's twenty-first birthday in 1975 took a "legal age"/"grown up" tack.*

Several years later, the company began retailing appliances, which ultimately became a larger part of the store's sales than televisions and audio systems. For that matter, appliance sales were bigger than record sales. The company changed its name to Cohen's in 1989 and thrived in Montgomery and the surrounding area, fending off the intrusion of "big box" retailers.

Michael Cohen credited the store's service to customers as the primary reason for its ongoing success. A quarter-century after the onset of the new millennium,

*Below, family business: Michael, David, and Raymond Cohen in a 1994 ad for The Record Shop. Right, someone in the newspaper's ad department made an amusing typo in the Allman Brothers name.*

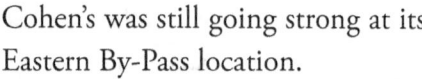

**Record Specials**

Our Regular $5.98

**NOW 3.50**

Entire Stovk:

- **The Osmonds**
- **Grand Funk**
- **Emerson, Lake And Palmer**
- **Almond Brothers**
- **John Denver**
- **Charlie Pride**
- **Porter Waggoner**
- **Johnny Cash**

**"Music Keeps The World In Harmony"**
Come Pick Up Your Favorites During This Big 3 Days of Savings

Cohen's was still going strong at its Eastern By-Pass location.

NORMANDALE'S 25TH ANNIVERSARY EVENTS began in March 1979, and several sidewalk sales were presented throughout the year. Gail Farrell of *The Lawrence Welk Show* and gospel singer Ron Anderson made appearances at Culp Piano & Organ.

However, Fannin's men's store announced its move to Montgomery Mall. And the business outlook for Normandale's future abruptly worsened when the Loveman's department store chain filed for Chapter 11 reorganization bankruptcy in 1979.

As the 1970s closed, Normandale changed its ownership and began to adjust its image, but Aronov Realty stayed on board for a short time as management. "We could tell that things were changing," Owen Aronov reflected, "Indoor malls were becoming popular, so from a business standpoint, we sold Normandale at the right time."

POTENTIAL INVESTORS TO SAVE Loveman's could not be found. Normandale's anchor store closed its doors for the final time at the end of the business day on Saturday, April 5, 1980.

The last day was particularly melancholic for Mildred Amos, who had been a housewife when she was hired by Loveman's in 1954. Amos was transferred to the credit

department in 1960, and worked her way up to become the store's credit manager and head cashier in 1965. She was the only worker who had been at the Montgomery Loveman's since it opened.

The loss of Loveman's left the rest of the shopping center's merchants reeling. Some would relocate to the newer indoor malls or open additional stores in the malls while trying to revitalize Normandale. Others simply went out of business.

"Like a lot of kids, I remember Santa in the upper window at Loveman's," said Foster Dickson, "and I remember those escalators. But my main memory is how my mother was absolutely heartbroken when Loveman's closed. I didn't understand back then that it was an anchor store. The city buses that used to stop in front of Loveman's stopped running to that location."

Dickson witnessed some of the latter-day changes at Normandale, such as Woolworth's being converted into a branch of the Montgomery Public Library. By the time he was bicycling to the shopping center on an almost daily basis, W. T. Grant had become Hancock Fabrics. The A&P grocery became an Alabama Beverage Control "state store" in 1980, to the consternation of some nearby residents and other Normandale customers (an anti-liquor store petition drive had been held).

Dickson also recalled that Normandale's basement community center was converted to a teen dance club in the late 1970s. "My brother was old enough to go to it," he said. "I wasn't." The club was first known as the Down Funky Street Coffee House with informal entertainment such as folk music and poetry readings. In the early 1980s, it became a members-only teen club known as Gatsby's Underground. In 1982, a group met there to plan the Capri Community Film Society.

Since 1977, Normandale had been presenting a temporary attraction each Halloween, sponsored by the Capital City Jaycees and a local radio station.

"For several years, there was also a haunted house-type of place called the 'Fright Factory' that would be set up in one of the empty stores in the arcade," said Dickson.

IN LATE 1980, THE architects Tiller, Butner and Rosa announced a major renovation and beautification initiative for the shopping center. The firm's spokesman was Joe Slaton, who was trying with longtime Normandale official Meredith Harrell to keep the shopping center active as an important retail landmark in central Alabama. Harrell said the canopies over the walkways would be replaced, and coach lights and other improvements would be added. He said that the Aronov company was aggressively looking for a replacement tenant for the now-empty Loveman's building.

Harrell left his position soon after the renovations were announced but remained with the Aronov conglomerate. The new mall manager was Michele Whitehurst. Raymond Cohen and Harrell continued to lunch together on a regular basis, even after they had both departed from Normandale.

REVCO, A NATIONAL DRUG store chain, acquired Normandale Drugs in 1981. The business later became a Harco Drugs store. A Duff's Smorgasbord restaurant opened in 1982, utilizing part of the former Loveman's space. It didn't last long.

Other businesses that opened in Normandale in the same era included a Hush Puppies Shoes store, H&J Beauty Supply, and WZTN Radio.

A Chinese restaurant opened in the early 1980s and went through several name changes in quick succession settling on The Bamboo Garden. The restaurant did a brisk business for a number of years, apparently faring better than the average Normandale store in that period.

"Their hot-and-sour soup was the best in the city," said one longtime customer.

SEISMIC SHIFTS TO THE EAST 125

The
Tradition
Keeps Growing
At Normandale Mall

"Your community shopping place"

ABC STORE
BAMBOO GARDENS
BARRY'S TRAVEL CENTER
BASKINS-ROBBINS
GUILLOT HEARING AID CENTER
DR. IRVING BERN, DENTIST
CAPITAL CITY LAUNDRY
CAPTAIN'S IMPORTS
COATES OPTICAL LABORATORY
ROOSEVELT A. DANIEL D.D.S.
DE SHIELDS-LARSON & WALKERS SHOES
DRAPERY OUTLET
FASHION WORKS
FINAL TOUCH BEAUTY SALON
1ST CHURCH OF CHRIST SCIENTISTS
HANCOCK FABRICS
H&O BEAUTY SUPPLY
MONTGOMERY CITY LIBRARY

MARK HALL CARD SHOP
MEL'S PHOTO SHOP & COMPUTERS
BRENNER'S LUGGAGE & GIFTS
NATIONAL MULTIPLE SCLEROSIS SOCIETY
NORMANDALE GULF SERVICE
GOUDY'S COVER PLASTIC & T-SHIRTS
OFFICE OF JUDGE OF PROBATE
PARKER-SLEDGE HARDWARE
CENTRAL BANK
REVCO DRUGS
ROPER'S JEWELERY
SEBRING BARBER & BEAUTY SHOP
STYLE ART BEAUTY SHOP
DRS. JOHN & MARK VERES, D.P.M.
THE VILLAGE STORE
WINN DIXIE
LIGER'S BAKERY
YUTMEYER'S PHOTOGRAPHY

✱ NORMANDALE MALL

NORMANBRIDGE ROAD at PATTON AVE.
(205-288-6075)

*Despite store closings, the retail center soldiered on. The above is a 1986 roster of merchants.*

As Normandale adjusted to changing demographics and area retail trends, the shopping center's promotions still included sidewalk sales. But by the middle of the 1980s some ads (see page 125) consisted of dealer listings and not-so-subliminal hints about patronizing the original mega-shopping center in central Alabama. Some annual ad layouts looked similar to each other.

1981

### Fabulous '50s Extravaganza

1982

All Day Saturday, June 12, at Normandale Mall
Welcoming Radio AM-10 to New Studios
* Classic Cars * Classic Music
* Sidewalk Sale * Radio Remote
* Jitterbug and Twist Contests
* **Favorite Radio Personalities
From Montgomery's Past**
*Don Jones, Tom Collins, Penn Scott, Bill Duke, Danny O'Day and Others!*

* **Prizes for Best '50s Era Costumes**
* **Good Ole Rock 'n Roll Music All Day**
* **Exciting Values Throughout the Mall**

normandale mall

normandale mall
SELECT MERCHANTS    SUPERIOR SERVICE

1982

It's **Halloween** at
**normandale mall**

SIDEWALK SALE SATURDAY — Fabulous Values Throughout
the Mall . . . Fright Factory Open Sat. 2-5:30 & 7:30 'Til ? . . .
Register for Free Car at Radio Station WZTN Booth!

1983

# Halloween

## SIDEWALK SALE

### GREAT BARGAINS IN GREAT STORES

SATURDAY
10-6

Come Visit the Capitol City Jaycees
7th ANNUAL FRIGHT FACTORY

normandale mall
SELECT MERCHANTS    SUPERIOR SERVICE

# The Ongoing Endgame

# 13

The dearth of viable stores continued to plague Normandale, as more retailers moved elsewhere or simply shut their doors.

Following the Loveman's closure, the front line grocery store became the anchor unit by default. Over its history, it changed from a Kwik Chek to a Winn-Dixie to a Calhoun Foods store to a Mega-Meats store, which closed in 2017.

Remaining in Normandale longer than most of their business peers, DeShields-Larson Shoes and the Lou Herman-owned stores fought the good fight. The Village Store branched out locally to Montgomery Mall and Eastdale Mall as well as Northside Mall in Dothan. Teens 'N Tweens was also a tenant in Montgomery Mall.

Later Herman-owned stores had names like the Wearhouse, David Michael's, Fashion Works, and Penelope Allen. Some were located in Normandale.

A branch of the Montgomery County Probate Court opened in the mid-1980s, as Normandale's tenant list shifted from exclusively retail stores to alternate lessees such as government offices.

The two Dexter Interiors stores closed in 1985. "My mother loved the stores," Lisa Segall detailed, "although my father—and my aunt and uncle, who owned the stores with them—would have liked to close them sooner. My mother won out because she had

cancer, and my father felt she needed the stores *psychologically.* The downtown store had closed maybe a year or so before that."

IN 1989, NORMANDALE WAS the headquarters for the filming of *The Long Walk Home,* a movie about the Montgomery Bus Boycott starring Sissy Spacek and Whoopi Goldberg. The former Loveman's was the temporary home of the movie crew's general offices, and the former ABC store housed the art department and a studio. Some interior scenes were shot on the premises.

The shopping center already had a plethora of

*Vintage Montgomery bus used in 1989 movie.*

vacancies, so a lot of the movie props were stored in empty stores. One could occasionally spot an old Montgomery city bus (painted in 1950s light green, white, and yellow colors) in the Nomandale parking lot.

Foster Dickson, then in his early teens, recalled his involvement as an extra in the movie:

"A friend and I went over and watched filming on the south end of Thomas Avenue one day. They were filming somebody walking into the house; it was pretty dull, frankly. But it was also enlightening to see how filming worked, that it took so long and so much standing around to get just a few seconds of footage. My friend Heather and I hung around most of the day. She was a pretty blonde, so some of the guys were hitting on her. That made me want to leave.

"Later that summer, we were finishing a show of *Mame* at the Montgomery Little Theater, and someone came into the dressing room saying that the *Long Walk Home* crew needed extras on set for a scene downtown. I was fourteen at the time, and my brother was nineteen. We went down there to be in the scene. They were in that alley off of North Court Street, filming the final triumphant scene where the 'good guys' stand firm against the yelling crowd of white racists. I played one of those yelling white guys, and you can see the back of my head in the movie.

"Beyond that, I remember being mad that they cut my hair. I went to private school and we had a hair rule, so the summer was the only time I could let it grow. We hadn't called our parents to say what we were doing, so they expected my brother and me home before midnight, and we came wandering in about 4 a.m. Got in trouble, of course.

"The next day, I walked up to Normandale to pick up our paychecks in the movie's offices. We were due $35 each, which was pretty good money in the late 1980s. My brother stayed home and made me get his check too. When I got there, other boys were sitting in the little makeshift lobby. I assumed they were picking up checks too.

"But then a casting person came out and said, 'All right, everybody come on back.' I sat there, because I didn't think it had anything to do with me, but the lady said, "Are you coming?" I told her no, that I was just waiting on a check. She said to come on and audition. For what, I had no idea. They had groups of white teenage boys auditioning for the scene in the bus when they harass the lone black girl. I didn't make the cut, but when I saw the movie later, I was glad I didn't."

When the movie crew and actors finished the on-location filming, a classified newspaper ad announced the sale of movie props on August 5 in the Normandale Mall arcade. According to the ad text, the items included "cars, t-shirts, everything," which included the movie prop buses.

Randall Williams was a long-time member of the board of directors of the Montgomery Improvement Association, the organization that ran the bus boycott. He recalls that the MIA delegated him and board member Joe Caver to negotiate with the movie producers to obtain the three 1950s city buses used in making the movie. The MIA gave one to Troy University to be included in the Rosa Parks museum that Troy was then building downtown where the Empire Theatre had been, in front of which Parks was arrested in 1955.

Bus Two, the only one that actually ran, ended up as the replica bus that the City of Montgomery restored and uses today in parades and on special occasions. The third bus was used for parts for the other two. (The Ford Museum in Detroit claims to have the actual bus that Parks was on at the time she was arrested.)

ADVERTISING TO PROMOTE NORMANDALE continued, including dealer listing ads in the early 1990s. Some of the ads had a "come home" theme, in an attempt to woo former customers who were shopping elsewhere.

In early 1991 a newspaper ad sponsored by the Normandale Merchants' Association (still active) welcomed three new tenants—the Popcorn Shoppe, Normandale Coin Laundry & Dry Cleaners, and Normandale Beauty Supply.

...

of shopping centers, died of heart failure on December 12, 1991, ten days shy of his seventy-second birthday. Tributes were received from across the country as well as from local civic and business leaders, including from the longtime Montgomery mayor Emory Folmar.

Courtesy of Alabama Business Hall of Fame

Ironically, though Aronov had attended the University of Alabama for only two years, he had served on the school's Board of Trustees. He was inducted into the Alabama Business Hall of Fame in Tuscaloosa in 1992.

IN THE MID-1990S, PLANS were being made to convert portions of Normandale to a "mall magnet

That summer, the Alabama Department of Public Health moved temporarily into the former Loveman's, Francis Cafeteria/Culp Piano & Organ, and other vacant retail spaces. The original plans envisioned a twelve-to-eighteen month occupancy during a renovation of the State Office Building downtown, where ADPH had been located.

But during the department's Normandale residency a decision was made to relocate the ADPH Central Office to the new RSA Tower building when that 22-story structure was completed in downtown Montgomery. The state agency remained in Normandale for several years.

AARON ARONOV, A LEGENDARY figure in real estate, particularly the development

high school" as part of the Montgomery Public Schools system. Space that was occupied by the State Health Department was to be converted to educational facilities after the Health Department moved into the RSA Tower. The project wasn't retail business-oriented, but it was innovative.

However, just after 5 a.m. on Wednesday, March 6, 1996, a killer tornado roared across south and east Montgomery, demolishing much of the arcade portion of Normandale and severely damaging the former Loveman's store. The storm also took down the 800-foot tall WCOV transmission tower several blocks away. Two persons in a mobile home in east Montgomery were killed.

Some sixteen years after Loveman's closed, the devastation caused by the twister was another gut punch regarding Normandale's viability.

One Public Health official told an interviewer he was grateful the tornado struck when the shopping center was unoccupied. The ADPH closed for two days for cleanup, then reopened in a "basic services" mode. The move into the RSA Tower ultimately took place over a six-week period in the spring of 1997.

Winn-Dixie repaired its Normandale store and was back in business on Thursday, May 9.

Imposing barriers displaying huge "No Trespassing" signs were erected at the entrances to the

arcade, much of which had been reduced to rubble.

The plans for a magnet school at Normandale were cancelled. Some years later, the same concept was implemented at the Montgomery Mall, which had also experienced decline.

The year of the end of Normandale's "glory days" may be debated but the shopping city's decline was long obvious as its businesses came and went.

Perhaps not surprisingly, the former Loveman's store housed a flea market at one point.

In 2018, the Alabama division of the Easterseals charity issued an illustrated Christmas ornament showing Santa Claus in the upper right-facing display window of Loveman's. It was based on a painting by artist Barbara Binford Davis.

The last of the businesses in Normandale that had flourished in the 1950s and 1960s was the bank on the western end of the front line. It had gone through numerous ownership changes and name changes by its closure in 2023.

**ATTENTION:**
**Normandale**
**Harco**
**Customers**

Your prescriptions can be filled at any Harco Super Drug while the Normandale store is closed, due to the tornado.

HARCO
**55 YEARS**
OF CARING

# 14

# Summation and Outro

"I think Normandale came along at exactly the right time for it to be a success," said David Robertson. "The post-war economy was booming, and there was a lot of new emphasis on buying for entire families in those days. There were those *Redbook* 'Easy Living' promotions that were presented by the Normandale folks—those events were good examples of what stores were trying to do.

"There were new products like plastic radios and clock radios for bedside tables. Those came into the marketplace in that time period and were extremely popular. You also had something new in the marketplace called 'conspicuous consumption'—people buying things to impress their friends. A lot of that was seen in automobile sales—two-tone finishes and carports. The body styles on some models changed radically from year to year.

"Grills for cookouts were a new item. Folding aluminum chairs for relaxing outdoors. Appliances in colors instead of just white—Paul (Jr.) still has a yellow refrigerator. There had been a movement towards indoor pets that started in the 1940s and 1950s, so Woolworth's in Normandale sold tropical fish, parakeets, and hamsters.

"In 2022, I had put an image of Santa in the Loveman's window on Facebook. It brought joyous memories to many people, so I felt that additional images of the shopping center would be of interest to a great number of people in the Montgomery area and to people who had grown up here and moved away."

As for the reasons Normandale is so fondly remembered by so many people, Michael Cohen opined that the courteous relationships of Normandale businesses with each other were reflected in the stores' service to customers.

"I think there was a lot of camaraderie, with all of the merchants," he said. "They were 'buddies,' and it was kind of like *Cheers*—everybody knew everybody, and it was like a team effort. Even if you competed with each other for business, you still wanted everybody to succeed. These days, it's kind of like 'Every man for himself.'

"I heard stories from my dad about Normandale when it first opened—big business people from all over the United States came here to see it, because they wanted to replicate it somewhere else. To me, it's still fascinating that Montgomery, Alabama, had something that somebody in California wanted to check out. I think that was an incredible legacy."

"I THINK MY FATHER was close to almost all of the merchants," Owen Aronov said wistfully. "As a child, I used to love going to Normandale with him, because he would say hello to every single merchant. He truly cared for each of them, and wanted each store to do as well as it possibly could. And they knew he was genuinely interested in their business. He would walk in and spend time with each tenant and would ask 'What can we do to help you?' He would discuss upcoming promotions and merchandise."

Owen agreed with Michael Cohen's observations regarding the Normandale merchants' comradeship. "It was synergistic," he said. "Almost all of the merchants were doing well. They were like part of our family, and those were very happy times."

MEMORIES FROM THE LATE Jane Laseter were probably typical for the untold number of Baby Boomers who came of age at Normandale. For many, the "shopping city on a hillock" was a major and permanent influence on their respective lifestyles. Laseter's recollections included:

"Cherry Cokes at the lunch counter in Woolworth's.

"Going to Kwik Chek with my mom. Strangely, at one time, the floor was carpeted.

"In 1969, my dad took me to the Central Bank next to the drugstore, where we opened my first checking account.

"My brother Ted worked at the Baskin-Robbins Ice Cream in approximately 1972.

"Buying albums at the Record Shop.

"On special occasions and some Sundays, we would go eat at the Francis Cafeteria. I was always excited about that, because they had any color of Jello a kid could want!"

THIS BOOK WAS DAVID Robertson's idea.

Finding appropriate photos from the Paul Robertson estate's gargantuan assortment of negatives proved to be an arduous task for his heirs, but at least his collection was in boxes and bags that were labeled Portraits, Weddings, Commercial/Aerial, Schools, and Debutante/Mystic Balls.

A number of individuals in the Robertsons' assortment of Normandale images could not be

absolutely, positively identified, but we used some of those photos anyway. Paul Robertson's photo of the woman seated in the millinery section of a Normandale clothing store is an example of the elusive identities we encountered. David and I both thought she might be Agnes Baggett, who served in Alabama state government for decades as secretary of state, state treasurer, and state auditor. Mary Jo Scott and Amelia Chase at the Alabama

*Left, Alabama stateswoman Agnes Baggett— State of Alabama. Below, her again? We don't know.*

Department of Archives and History thought otherwise—differences in nose shape and eyebrows—so I'll defer to their judgment, but such mysteries are always intriguing.

The John Engelhardt Scott collection at the Department of Archives and History was, as noted in the photographers' introductory profiles, admirably and efficiently organized and accessible.

But there's still that mysterious RFK photo that dates from 1959 . . .

IN HIS 2003 BOOK *Once Upon a Town: The Miracle of the North Platte Canteen,* author Bob Greene took readers on a concise chronological excursion in search of the "business district" of North Platte, Nebraska. Perhaps not surprisingly, the brief tour started downtown, stopped at an indoor shopping mall that seemed to be losing tenants, and terminated at a bustling Super Walmart that was open 24/7. Greene's chronology of North Platte's "business district" is applicable to thousands of burgs all across America.

Obviously, many larger, *non-enclosed* open-air original-style shopping centers like Normandale could also fit into a storyline of the evolution of American retail business in specific communities. Such a citation would make for another stop (at least, in towns that were large enough to have had original-style shopping centers). The revised equitable chronological order would be downtown / open-air shopping center / enclosed mall / Super Walmart (and maybe a few other big-box stores).

But in its time, Normandale was indeed a lifestyle lodestone—a gigantic, innovative and highly successful enterprise that served the needs of hundreds of thousands of shoppers.

SOME YEARS AGO—LONG BEFORE the idea for this book germinated—I happened to be in Montgomery on "investigative guitar business" in the general area of my old neighborhood, so I took some extra time for a slow cruise down familiar residential streets like Beaumont Drive and Avalon Lane.

It wasn't surprising that Normandale also beckoned from a distance of about four blocks. It had been many years since I'd shopped there, and I recalled that it had changed owners more than once (and later confirmed such).

I guess I should have expected the "shopping city" to be in bad shape, but the condition of the once-thriving mega-center was jaw-dropping. I decided then and there that if I ever wrote *anything* about Normandale's history—be it an article, a commentary, or maybe a chapter in a book—I would take an almost-exclusively nostalgic bent. No detailed documentation of a so-called "decline" would be included. Even though such a doleful era was part of the history, I wasn't going to extensively research and chronicle Normandale's deterioration. The morbid time period *did* have to be addressed, of course, but "downer" particulars weren't going to be historically dissected and analyzed. The title of this book suggests that its narrative and images focus on the better days.

AS I SLOWLY DROVE around the perimeter of the once-vibrant retail showplace, I noted the permanently mysterious parabola of the grocery store roofline—a worn yet still modernist sentinel gazing out over a large parking lot containing only a handful of cars.

I stopped my car and got out only once. The display windows on the ground floor of the former Loveman's appeared to have vacant, wide-open spaces behind them. I got out and pressed my nose against the exterior of the plate glass, as many window shoppers would have, starting in September 1954.

While cylindrical interior support columns were still in place on the first floor, the overall view of the interior was a vast and empty panorama. The only visual aberration was the now-broken-down escalator, its two mechanisms forming a decrepit and forlorn X-shaped monolith in the center of the store, surrounded by thousands of square feet of nothing.

I glumly shuffled back to my car. The temperature was cool, and a light breeze wafted through the parking lot. The sky was bright and cloudless. Call it "windbreaker weather."

Despite the relatively comfortable conditions, I shivered as I turned on the ignition.

Paul Robertson Sr.

# 15

# Glory Days: Legendary Lists and Logos (and 20/20 Hindsight)

STORES, MEDICAL AND FINANCIAL OFFICES, AND RESTAURANTS (OPENED SEPTEMBER 1954), ALPHABETICAL ORDER

- Capitol Clothing
- City Florist
- Clay Crumpton's Laundromat
- Darby & Sons Cleaners
- DeShields-Larson Shoes
- Doctors' Building offices (fully occupied in November, 1954)
- Ellis Optical
- Flack's Ltd.
- Francis Cafeteria (opened in November, 1954)
- Kwik Chek
- Lee's Cut-Rate Drugs
- Liger's Bakery
- Lou Herman's
- Louise's Beauty Salon
- Loveman's
- Mel's Photo Shop
- Montgomery Shoe Factory
- Normandale Barber Shop
- Normandale Delicatessen
- Pauline Wilkins Candies
- Parker-Sledge Hardware
- Sauls Footwear
- Roslyn Eagle Furniture
- Town & Country
- Toyland
- Western Auto
- F. W. Woolworth
- Wright Interiors

NON-ORIGINAL STORES, INCLUDING "ARCADE STORES" (OPENED IN 1957), ALPHABETICAL ORDER

(Doctors, dentists, etc., who occupied the Doctors' Building over the Francis Cafeteria—and later, Culp Piano & Organ—in November 1954 are also included in this list, in alphabetical order of surname. The lineup of original physicians and staff wasn't complete by September's grand opening. Later doctors and dentists also listed.)

- Alabama Department of Economic and Community Affairs
- A&P
- Alabama Beverage Control ("ABC") Store
- Alabama Department of Public Health
- Al Levy's

- A. Nachman's
- Baker's
- Bamboo Garden
- Barry's Travel Center
- Baskin-Robbins
- BBVA Compass Bank
- Beauty Supply Unlimited
- Dr. Irving Bern
- Dr. Jeffrey Bern
- Bill's Beauty Shop
- Brenner's Shoe Factory
- Burger Ranch
- Calhoun Foods
- Dr. E. Fred Campbell
- Captain's Imports
- Central Bank
- Christian Science Reading Room
- Cloth World
- Coventry Hall
- CMC Drapery Outlet
- Coates Optical
- Compass Bank
- Culp Piano & Organ
- Dad 'N' Lad
- Dr. Roosevelt Daniel DDS
- Dexter Interiors
- Diana Shops
- Down Funky Street Coffee House
- Drapery Outlet
- Duff's Smorgasbord
- Dr. Jesse Ellington
- Evening Out Formal Wear & Professional Alterations
- Dr. William Farrar
- Dr. J. H. Farrior
- The Fashion Tree
- Fashion Works
- Fannin's
- Gatsby's Underground
- W. T. Grant

- Dr. Robert Guillot
- H & O Beauty Supply
- Half-Price Shoe Store
- Hancock Fabrics
- Harco Drugs
- Hush Puppies Shoes
- Jarman Shoes
- Joy's Restaurant
- Junior Vogue
- Knit N' Stitch
- Lord's Carpets
- Magic Rentals
- Mandarin House
- Mark Hall
- The Maternity Shop
- McAdams Carpet
- McLendon Athletic Center
- MedCo
- Mega-Meats
- Miller's
- Montgomery Public Library
- Montgomery County Probate Court
- Movie Gallery
- Mr. A's Flack's
- The Name Dropper
- New England Book and Pipe
- Norman Jewelers
- Normandale Beauty Supply
- Normandale Coin Laundry & Dry Cleaners
- Normandale Optical Dispensary
- Normandale Restaurant
- Normandale Union 76
- Pant-A-Rama
- People's Bank & Trust
- Pizza Presto
- PNC Bank
- Popcorn Shoppe
- The Record Shop
- Revco Drugs
- Richards ("Clothes for the Lion-Hearted")

- Roper's Jewelry
- Sound Shop
- Southern Technical College
- Sports Palace
- Stanhope Outlet Store
- Style Art Beauty Salon
- Teens 'N Tweens
- Thom McAn Shoes
- Unclaimed Furniture
- U.S.A. Financial Services
- Drs. John & Mark Veres, DPM
- Video Xpress
- The Village Store
- Virginia Dare
- Walker's Hush Puppies
- Dr. Conrad Walters
- Dr. Ed Webb
- Dr. John White
- Dr. Kathleen Wickman
- Winn-Dixie
- Western Auto
- WZTN Radio
- The Yardstick
- Yutmeyer Photography

## LOGOS

Logos from all "eras" of Normandale history are shown here in alphabetical order. In some cases, they were found in a composite ad for the entire shopping city, and certain stores may have been in business at the shopping center only briefly.

Several business logos "evolved" cosmetically over the years. Some stores, like Wright's Interiors, didn't seem too concerned with permanent logos, as the layout of the store's name in newspaper ads frequently changed. Other evolving designs include Mel's Photo Shop, People's Bank & Trust and the logos for Normandale Shopping City/Center itself.

That said, an "official" logo representing the entire shopping center didn't really appear until 1957. However, more than one early ad displayed the Normandale name in plain block letters, superimposed over a line drawing of the original frontline stores. As noted in Chapter 6, the original logo for the expanded shopping center was inspired by the three pennants at the entrance of the breezeway to the arcade. Ten designs are shown here:

**Normandale Shopping City logos, numbered in date order of introduction**

## Merchant Logos

# A.Nachman

**ARONOV**
**REALTY COMPANY, Inc.**
42 S. COURT ST.                    MONTGOMERY, ALA.
PHONE 3-0532

*Baker's*

The
Bamboo
Garden
Oriental
Restaurant

*Barry's*
Travel
Center

**Brenner's Shoe Factory**
*"Serving Montgomery Since 1910"*
Normandale Mall

*Bronson's*
*Normandale Arcade*

*Capitol Clothing Store*

*City*
*Florist*

in Normandale

*Cloth World*

**Coventry Hall**
107 Normandale Arcade

**CULP'S** PIANO & ORGAN CO.
Normandale                    281-6117

*Darby*
*& Sons*

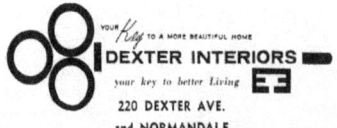

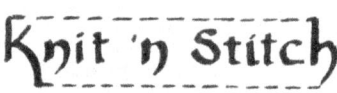

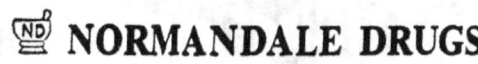

SAULS FOOTWEAR
IN NORMANDALE

SHAKEY'S Pizza PARLOR
Ye Public House

Shakey's

SOUND SHOP
Normandale Shopping Center

SPORTS PALACE

STANHOPE
OUTLET STORE

Style-Art BEAUTY SALON

TEENS 'N TWEENS
NORMANDALE

Teens 'n Tweens

Town & Country

TOYLAND
NORMANDALE

★ ★ ★ VIDEO X-PRESS ★ ★ ★

the Village store
NORMANDALE

THE WEARHOUSE

WESTERN AUTO

WINN DIXIE

F. W. WOOLWORTH

Woolworth

WRIGHT
interiors
Normandale

WRIGHT INTERIORS
Normandale Shopping Center

WRIGHT INTERIORS
Normandale Shopping Center

WRIGHT interiors
IN NORMANDALE

Wright Interiors, Inc.
NORMANDALE SHOPPING CITY        AM 3-2527

Yardstick
FASHION FABRICS

YARDSTICK, INC.
Normandale

young fashions

ZALE'S JEWELERS

ZALES
The Diamond Store

142

# SOURCES

## PERIODICALS

"3 Women Convicted In Shoplifting Cases." *Alabama Journal*, December 7, 1960

"1,300 Feet Glass Used In Center." *Montgomery Advertiser*, September 9, 1954

"4,000 Visit Normandale for Opening of Addition." *Montgomery Advertiser*, March 8, 1957

"10,000 Attend Kickoff of Hank Williams Show." *Alabama Journal*, September 21, 1954

"A Road Trip Into The History of American Camping With Ford's 'Station Wagon Living.' *Thervatlas.com*

"Aaron Aronov Shaped Dream of Normandale." *Montgomery Advertiser*, September 9, 1954

"All The Family's Welcome at Normandale." *Alabama Journal*, September 1, 1955

Andrews, Margie. "Rev. Johnston Minister of Local New Church." *Alabama Journal*, August 27, 1955; "Normandale Methodists to Consecrate Building." *Montgomery Advertiser*, January 5, 1957

"Anniversary Celebrated At Normandale."*Alabama Journal*, August 24, 1961

"Antique Autos, Rare Stamps Entered In Hobby show." *Montgomery Advertiser*, June 2, 1961

"Aronov Vision, Courage Resulted In Normandale." *Montgomery Advertiser*, August 25, 1960

"Attendant At Kiddie-Land Offers Aid for Parents." *Alabama Journal*, September 1, 1955

"Auditorium Set for Meetings At Normandale." *Alabama Journal*, August 28, 1958

Azbell, Joe. "Department Store Planned In New Normandale Center." *Montgomery Advertiser*, April 19, 1953; "Big Shopping Center Starts in Normandale." *Montgomery Advertiser*, December 13, 1953; "Normandale Makes Montgomery State Shopping Capital." *Montgomery Advertiser*, September 9, 1954

"Baptists to Build Church In Normandale." *Montgomery Advertiser*, December 2, 1952

'BRHS Band Is Rated 'Tops' Tuesday In Hank Williams Parade." *Alexander City Outlook*, September 24, 1954

Cannon, Jimmy. "That's The Way Dusty Makes His Living." *Birmingham News*, September 30, 1954

"Capitol Clothing Plans Branch in Normandale." *Montgomery Advertiser*, April 18, 1954

"Center Fulfills Hopes Held By Aaron Aronov." *Montgomery Advertiser*, August 28, 1958

"City's New Center Opens Today." *Montgomery Advertiser*, March 19, 1957

"Cleo Moore, Camera Fan, Visits Mel's Photo Shop." *Montgomery Advertiser*, April 8, 1955

"Coffee House Returns." *Montgomery Advertiser*, June 14, 1981

"Completion Date Set In '57 for 17 Stores." *Alabama Journal*, December 12, 1956

"Construction Contract Awarded On First Unit of Multi-Million Normandale Baptist Church." *The Montgomery Advertiser*, January 2, 1956

"Dedication Service Set for Normandale Church." *Alabama Journal*, November 3, 1956

"DeShields-Larson Expands Selection of Quality Shoes." *Montgomery Advertiser*, August 25, 1960

"DeShields-Larson Has Shoes to Set Your Feet A-Dancing." *Montgomery Advertiser*, August 27, 1959.

"Design, Construction, Cooling Contributed to Center's Success." Montgomery Advertiser, March 7, 1958

"Dombrowski Quits Normandale Post." *Montgomery Advertiser*, December 1, 1954

"Dombrowski to Manage Normandale." *Montgomery Advertiser*, September 9, 1954

"During '58 Normandale Becomes Shopping CITY," *Alabama Journal*, August 28, 1958

"Easy Living At Normandale." *Montgomery Advertiser*, May 1, 1958

"'Easy Living' Shown At Normandale." *Montgomery Advertiser*, March 17, 1960

"Electric Doors to Aid New Bank's Customers" *Alabama Journal*, January 23, 1957

"Exclusive Shop Features Home Furnishings of The Very Finest Quality." *Montgomery Advertiser/Alabama Journal*, September 9, 1954

"Famous Dallas, Texas Firm Land-Planned Normandale." *Montgomery Advertiser/Alabama Journal*, September 9, 1954

Fields, Monique. "Magnet Mall Plans Suffer Setback." *Montgomery Advertiser*, March 28, 1996, and "Mall Won't Host Magnet Program," April 5, 1996

"First New Bank In 50 Years Here to Open In Normandale." *Montgomery Advertiser/Alabama Journal*, December 30, 1956

"Flack's Store Features Exclusive Designs." *Montgomer Advertiser*, September 9, 1954

"Ford's New Thunderbird." *Birmingham News*, October 5, 1954

"Forest Hills to Get New Center." *Alabama Journal*, January 11, 1956

"Fourth Bank Expected Here." *Alabama Journal*, July 13, 1956

"Free, Fast, Cool Ride Available At Normandale." *Montgomery Advertiser, July 1, 1960*

"From A Hay Field to A Market Place for Many Thousands." *Montgomery Advertiser/Alabama Journal*, March 3, 1957

"Gail Farrell to Attend Culp Piano & Organ Co. Grand Opening in Normandale." *Montgomery Advertiser*, November 9, 1972

Gates, Darryl. "Normandale Shopping City merchants say customers pleased with renovation." *Montgomery Advertiser/Alabama Journal*, March 29, 1981

Gerome, John. "Health Agency Moving." *Montgomery Advertiser*, July 30, 1991

"Giant Party to Mark First Birthday of Normandale," *Montgomery Advertiser*, September 1, 1955

"Giant Santa Greets Normandale Kids." *Montgomery Advertiser*, November 24, 1962

"Grand Ole Opry Performers to Ride In Mammoth Hank Williams Day Parade." *Montgomery Advertiser*, September 20, 1954

Greenhaw, Wayne. "Aronov: A Businessman Who Gave Heart, Soul to the Community. *Alabama Journal*, December 23, 1991

"Grocery Store Leaves Anchor Spot In Normandale." *Montgomery Advertiser*, April 5, 2017

Greuner, Jordan. "Movie Gives Normandale Renewed Life." *Alabama Journal*, April 23, 1989

"Half Million Enjoy Services of Giant Center." *Montgomery Advertiser*, September 1, 1955

Hamilton, Michael. "Normandale Marks Twentieth Anniversary." *Montgomery Advertiser*, September 8, 1974

"Hank Williams Memorial Day Proclaimed Sept. 21 By Persons." *Alexander City Outlook*, August 13, 1954

"Hank's Room Will Be Open to Public." *Montgomery Advertiser, September 20, 1954*

"Hopalong Jr." *Alabama Journal*, September 1, 1955

Hutsell, James K. "Jack Turner Is Talked for Role As Hank Williams." *Alabama Journal*, August 24, 1954

"Jehle Brothers Contractors for Normandale Center." *Montgomery Advertiser/Alabama Journal*, September 9, 1954

Kemp, Kathy. "'The Long Walk Home' Takes Last Step, Finally Opens Today." *Birmingham Post-Herald*, December 21, 1990

Lackeos, Nick. "This Is Normandale." *Alabama Journal*, May 6, 1980; "Normandale Center Getting Face-Lift." *Alabama Journal*. November 25, 1980; "Robertson Captures Life's Moments on Film." *Montgomery Advertiser*, November 29, 1987

"Largest Christmas Tree Lighted At Normandale." *Alabama Journal*, December 1, 1956

Lee, Gerry. "Dusty Coming Home Saturday for His 'Day'." *Montgomery Advertiser*, October 5, 1954

"Levy's First Founded Here In Mid-Twenties." *Alabama Journal*, August 15, 1963

Lewis, Danny. "Closing of Loveman's Brings End to Woman's 'Family Store' Career." *Montgomery Advertiser*, April 6, 1980

Logue, Mickey. "1954 World Series Hero Arrives This Afternoon." *Montgomery Advertiser*, October 8, 1954; "Montgomery Throws Out Welcome Mat for Dusty Rhodes." *Alabama Journal*, October 8, 1954

"Loveman's Synonymous With Normandale Center." *Alabama Journal*, August 27, 1959

"Loveman's Will Establish New Store in Montgomery's Normandale Area." Birmingham News, April 19, 1953

Lucci, Jo Anne. "Merchants Aid Blue and Gray." *Alabama Journal*, November 4, 1954

Martin, Virginia. "for Goblins and Ghosts—It's Opening Night." *Alabama Journal*, October 15, 1982

"Massive Christmas Tree Glows at Shopping Center." *Montgomery Advertiser*, December 1, 1956

McCluskey, Wanda. "Normandale to Have New Shop." November 24, 1974

"Merchants Association Looks to Convenience of Shoppers." *Montgomery Advertiser*, August 28, 1958

"Miss America Will Cut Ribbon for New Addition Thursday." *Montgomery Advertiser*, March 7, 1957

"Modern Center Will Be Built In Normandale." *Montgomery Advertiser*, April 19, 1953

"Modern Selling Techniques Key to Normandale Success." *Montgomery Advertiser*, August 23, 1962

"Montgomery Fair Celebrates Grand Opening on Thursday." *Montgomery Advertiser*, February 17, 1965

"Montgomery Hula Experts Hooping It Up." *Montgomery Advertiser*, October 1, 1958

"Montgomery's Little Theater Purchasing Historic Holy Comforter Church Building." *Montgomery Advertiser*,

November 26, 1958

Morton, John. "Smoocher Cleo Busts In Town to Help Movie." *Montgomery Advertiser,* April 5, 1955

"Mrs. America Visits Normandale." *Alabama Journal,* August 24, 1961

"No More Parking Problems." Montgomery Advertiser, August 28, 1958

"Normandale Bapist Church Receives Title to New Lot." *Montgomery Advertiser,* August 22, 1955

"Normandale's Beauty Grows Under Organized Programs." *Montgomery Advertiser*, August 28, 1958.

"Normandale Begins Celebration." *Alabama Journal,* August 22, 1963

"Normandale Begins Their Anniversary Celebration Today." *Montgomery Advertiser/Alabama Journal,* August 22, 1957

"Normandale Blends Shopping Ease With Fun for All." *Alabama Journal,* August 27, 1959

"Normandale Celebrates 8th Birthday." *Montgomery Advertiser*, August 23, 1962

"Normandale Celebrates Anniversary." *Alabama Journal,* August 28, 1958

"Normandale Contest Winners Are Named." *Alabama Journal,* May 19, 1953

"Normandale Celebrates Anniversary." *Montgomery Advertiser*, August 28, 1958

"Normandale Expansion Now Underway." *Alabama Journal,* August 22, 1956

"Normandale Hails New Bank Opening." *Alabama Journal,* January 23, 1957

"Normandale Is Convenient." *Alabama Journal,* August 22, 1956

"Normandale Land Tract Has Long, Colorful History." *Montgomery Advertiser/Alabama Journal,* September 9, 1954

"Normandale Marks Twentieth Year." *Montgomery Advertiser*, September 8, 1974

"Normandale Offers Shopping Ease." *Montgomery Advertiser,* August 25, 1960.

"Normandale Ready for You." *Montgomery Advertiser,* September 1, 1955

"Normandale Set for Party." *Montgomery Advertiser/Alabama Journal,* September 1, 1955

"Normandale Shopping Center Announces Winner of Chevrolet Automobile." Montgomery Advertiser, February 26, 1956

"Normandale Shopping Center to Be Fully Air-Conditioned." *Montgomery Advertiser/Alabama Journal,* September 9, 1954

"Normandale Teens 'N Tweens New Type of Store In State." *Alabama Journal,* August 22, 1957

"Normandale to Observe Second Birthday." *Montgomery Advertiser/Alabama Journal,* August 23, 1956

"Normandale Tree Will Be Officially Lighted Today." *Montgomery Advertiser,* Nobember 30, 1956

"Normandale Tries to Supply All Needs." Alabama Journal, August 22, 1956

"Normandale Shopping Center Will Open Playground Today." *Montgomery Advertiser,* June 24, 1955.

"No More Parking Problems." *Alabama Journal,* August 28, 1958

Owens, Wesley. "Montgomery Opens Arms to Ball-Hitting Son." *Montgomery Advertiser*, October 9, 1954; "More Than 10,000 Fans Join In Tribute to Dusty Rhodes." *Montgomery Advertiser,* October 10, 1954

"Operator of Flack's Limited Hails Normandale's Success." *Montgomery Advrtiser.* March 7, 1957

"Pauline Wilkins' Candy Masterpiece of Taste." *Montgomery Advertiser,* March 7, 1957

"Peoples Bank & Trust Company Opens Thursday," *Alabama Journal,* January 23, 1957

"Personal Interest Key At Normandale." *Montgomery Advertiser,* August 23, 1962

"Polio, Hank Williams Funeral, Gayden Trail Top City Stories." Montgomery Advertiser, December 31, 1953

"Rhodes Pinch Homer 4th In Series History." *Birmingham News,* September 30, 1954

Rountree, David. "Spillover Crowd Packs Funeral for Mr. Aronov." *Montgonery Advertiser,* December 23, 1991

"Second Birthday Cake Tops 1300-Pound Mark." *Montgomery Advertiser,* August 23, 1956

"Shoppers Still Are Amazed At Normandale's Magnitude." *Montgomery Advertiser,* September 1, 1955

"Shopping Center Gaining 3 New Firms in Late '61." *Montgomery Advertiser,* August 24, 1961

Smith, Matt. "Montgomery Real Estate Giant Dies of Heart Failure At 71." *Alabma Journal,* December 15, 1991; "Normandale Residents Glad Tornado Toll Wasn't Worse." *Montgomery Advertiser,* March 8, 1996.

Smith, Mildred. "Fair Eastbrook Opens Thursday." *The Montgomery Advertiser,* April 11, 1957

"Spirit of Cooperation Observed by Merchants." *Montgomery Advertiser-Alabama Journal,* August 23, 1956

"Store Managers At Center Have All Types of Callers." *Montgomery Advertiser,* September 1, 1955

"Suburban Living Reflected." *Montgomery Advertiser*, August 28, 1958

Taylor, Greg. "Normandale Facelift Slated." *Montgomery Advertiser/Alabama Journal.* August 31, 1980; "Shopping Center Gets Facelift." *Montgomery Advertiser/Alabama Journal,* August 8, 1982; "State Business Climate Gets 'A' in Magazine's National Survey." *Montgomery Advertiser,* October 11, 1981

Thames, Roger. "Hank Enshrined in Hillbilly Hearts." *Birmingham News,* September 22, 1954

Thames, Roger. "Hillbilly Entertainers Throng Capital to Honor Hank." *Birmingham News,* September 21, 1954

"Thousands Flock to Montgomery for Wiliams Memorial

Climax." *Alabama Journal*, September 21, 1954

"Thunderbird Display Opens At Loveman's." *Alabama Journal*, October 12, 1954

Till, Joyce. "Beauty Queen Snips Ribbon for Center." *Alabama Journal*, March 7, 1957

Tillotson, Jery. "Swine Flu Shots Begin October 18 In Montgomery." *Montgomery Advertiser*, October 10, 1976

"Toyland Draws Fascination of Adults As Well As Kids." *Montgomery Advertiser*, March 7, 1957

"Treasure Chest Special Event." *Montgomery Advertiser/Alabanma Journal*, August 22, 1957

"Unity of Stores Adds Charm to Queen of Centers." *Montgomery Advertiser*, March 3, 1957

Van Hoose, Alf. "'Bama Day In Old New York." *Birmingham News*, September 30, 1954

"Virginia Dare Shop, Doctors Building Youngest Members of Normandale Family." *Alabama Journal*, September 1, 1955

Witt, Elaine. "Montgomery Malls Try Renovation to Stay Alive." *Montgomery Advertiser*, January 11, 1987

Witt, Elaine. "Normandale Accelerated Movement of Shopping Centers to The Suburbs."*Montgomery Advertiser*, January 11, 1987

Wells, Martha. "Center Opens At Normandale." *Alabama Journal*, September 10, 1954

Wojnar, Rose, "Teen Nightclubs Provide Good, Clean Fun." *Mongomery Advertiser*, May 13, 1984

Woodress, Fred. "Will Jack Turner Portray Hank Williams In MGM Film?" *Birmingham Post-Herald*, November 1, 1954

"Woolworth Slates Opening of New Normandale Store." *Montgomery Advertiser*, Aust 8, 1957

"Worker Spots Stars at Normandale Mall." *Alabama Journal,*, May 15, 1989

"Year's End Denotes Period of Expansion At Normandale." *Montgomery Advertiser*, December 29, 1957

## ONLINE SITES

https://abandonedalabama.com
https://abhof.culverhouse.ua.edu
https://archives.alabama.gov
https://aronovrealty.com
https://www.newspapers.com
https://www.pintlalahistoricalassociation.com
http://thervatlascom
https://sabr.org
http://woolworthsmuseum.co.uk

## BOOKS

Escott, Colin & Florita, Kira, *Hank Williams: Snapshots from the Lost Highway*. Boston, Massachusetts. DaCapo Press, 2001.

Greene, Bob. *Once Upon a Town: The Miracle of the North Platte Canteen*. New York, New York. HarperCollins Publishers, 2003.

Tennille, Toni. *Toni Tennille—A Memoir*. Lanham, Maryland, Taylor Trade Publishing, 2016.

Best-selling author/lecturer Willie G. Moseley is the Senior Writer for *Vintage Guitar Magazine*. He lives in Hank Williams Territory. This is his eighteenth book.

# Index

www.ingramcontent.com/pod-product-compliance
Lightning Source LLC
Chambersburg PA
CBHW081659120626
46550CB00010B/2950